Teaching English Learners and Students with Learning Difficulties in an Inclusive Classroom

A Guidebook for Teachers

John Carr & Sharen Bertrando

Printed in the United States of America.

ISBN: 978-0-914409-67-0

Library of Congress Control Number: 2012933459

The book cover is printed on 30% recycled paper. The text paper is certified by the Sustainable Forest Initiative.

WestEd, a national nonpartisan, nonprofit research, development, and service agency, works with education and other communities to promote excellence, achieve equity, and improve learning for children, youth, and adults. WestEd has 16 offices nationwide, from Washington and Boston to Arizona and California. Its corporate headquarters are in San Francisco.

WestEd books and products are available through bookstores and online booksellers. WestEd also publishes its books in a variety of electronic formats.

To order books from WestEd directly, call our Publications Center at 888-293-7833 or visit us online at www.WestEd.org/bookstore.

For more information about WestEd:

Visit www.WestEd.org

Call 415-565-3000 or toll free 877-4-WestEd

Write WestEd

730 Harrison Street
San Francisco, CA 94107-1242

Editor: Noel White

Managing Editor: Joy Zimmerman

Design Director: Christian Holden

Graphic Designer: Fredrika Baer

Proofreader: Joan D. Saunders

Chief Executive Officer: Glen Harvey

Chief Program Officer: Gary Estes

Chief Policy and Communications Officer: Max McConkey

Publications Manager: Danny S. Torres

Publications Assistant: Tanicia Bell

Dedications

Drawing by John Carr's son, Tony, illustrating one of the key concepts discussed in this book.

I dedicate this book to my son, Natthaphon, nicknamed Tony, who has dual designation as an English learner with autism spectrum disorder, aural language processing difficulties, and dyscalculia. Beneath his educational labels, Tony is honest, caring, respectful, and humorous and loves learning new facts and "power words." He has aspirations of college, a good job, a fast car, and being a good husband and father. His primary interests are the weather, natural disasters, cars, airplanes (he took the controls of an airplane for his Boy Scout aviation merit badge), hiking, camping, and traveling the world. This guidebook is about the best way to teach Tony and similar students who want to learn so much despite their challenges. I also dedicate this book to the many teachers who work so hard, with so much skill and caring, to teach these students and help them realize their aspirations.

— John Carr

I dedicate this book to practitioners who are committed to being a part of the solution to the nation's educational crisis: ensuring that all students go beyond the basics to develop the innovative skills and creativity necessary to have personal choices in the workforce of the 21st century. As Plato wrote: "The direction in which education starts a man will determine his future life."

— Sharen Bertrando

Contents

Tools and Strategies

Acknowledgments

We were very fortunate to have the advice of a number of experts in content, English language development, and special education instruction during the development of this guidebook. Their generosity in formally reviewing the manuscript and offering numerous comments and suggestions resulted in many refinements that became part of the final product. We hope the guidebook reflects their collective wisdom.

Reviewers were:

Elizabeth Hughes, Assistant Professor, Duquesne University

Donald Kairott, consultant with WestEd, formerly with the California Department of Education

Janette Klingner, Professor, University of Colorado at Boulder

Marion Miller, Special Education Resource Development Specialist with the Center for Prevention and Early Intervention at WestEd

Marla Perez-Selles, Senior Research and Program Associate with Learning Innovations at WestEd

Kristin Reedy, Director of the Northeast Regional Resource Center at WestEd

Nancy Snodgrass, Bilingual Special Education Resource teacher, Turlock Unified School District

Dee Torrington, Beginning Teacher Support and Assessment trainer for special education and President-elect of California Association for Special Educators

Elizabeth Watkins, ELL and Minority Issues, Special Education Policy Division, Minnesota Department of Education

We thank Marion Miller for her contributions and literature research when we were conceptualizing this guidebook.

We welcome your feedback as well; please write to us at info@WestEd.org, or contact the authors directly using the email addresses included in our authors' bios.

Introduction

> **If students are not learning the way we teach them, we must teach them the way they learn.**
>
> — Kenneth Dunn

Diversity within the classroom is increasing as more English learners enter our education system and more students with special needs are welcomed into general education classrooms. In this guidebook, we offer a unified, doable approach for teachers to adapt to this increasing diversity of students in their classrooms.

Effective teachers continually explore and experiment with new ways to engage all students in successful learning; they see the changing demographics in their classrooms as a challenge to be met, not a problem to be avoided. They learn to tailor instruction to meet students "where they are" and to help them all progress toward the same set of academic standards. Each student is at a unique point of readiness to learn any lesson, each learns best in a unique way and has personal interests, so it is imperative that teachers find personalized ways to help each student be a successful learner.

The reality in a classroom of 30 students with diverse learning needs is that the teacher does not have time to teach each student individually. The teacher can have a positive impact on students by planning a lesson for all students, embedding very doable strategies from this book that are effective for all students, and then making *minor adjustments* for certain students.[1] The teacher might personalize a lesson by selecting one or a few concrete examples of a concept that taps into one student's interests (e.g., anything about airplanes and airports) and another's culture or primary language.

Diverse Ways of Teaching and Learning

for an **INDIVIDUAL** student

for a **TYPE** of student

for **ALL** students

This guidebook is intended to help teachers bring together and enhance effective practices that they may have learned previously. For teachers who have participated in professional development and read books and articles related to working with English learners or students with learning disabilities (what we refer to as learning *difficulties*), we expect that many of the strategies presented here are at least somewhat familiar. Our approach to teaching English learners and students with learning difficulties is in harmony with popular models such as Cognitive Academic Language Learning Approach (CALLA) and Sheltered Instruction Observation Protocol (SIOP).[2,3] These models involve teaching in the content areas in a manner that researcher Arieh Sherris calls "task-based," which "focuses on the knowledge, skills, and academic language within a content area."[4]

This guidebook proposes a very doable, practical, everyday approach backed by research and other evidence for effectively teaching diverse learners, particularly English learners and students with learning difficulties in the general education classroom or in an academic special education classroom. There is no expensive program to buy, no new materials that must be purchased, no rigid step-by-step directions for implementation, and no entirely new ways of teaching. Many teachers say they have used some or all of the strategies in this guidebook but have not used them often enough or sustained their use. We hope this guidebook will help teachers return to these effective strategies, make refinements in them, implement them more frequently, and continue building on them as the benefits to their teaching and to students become obvious.

This book is based on two prior guidebooks for science and mathematics teachers who have English learners in their classrooms.[5] A common thread among the strategies in the prior two guidebooks is making instruction visible and repeating key concepts so that the English learners who find it difficult to process oral English rapidly can access the content of the lesson and grade-level learning standards.

Howard Gardner and others have convinced us that there are multiple intelligences and that students have preferred learning styles and interests. It has been suggested that about two thirds of students in classrooms today have a preference for a visual and spatial style of learning, "thinking in pictures," and struggle with the words to describe those pictures.[6] Many students with learning difficulties are visual-spatial learners, hence many of the strategies that we recommend are particularly effective for visual-spatial learning. Workshop participants and a review of literature in special education have affirmed our belief that the strategies in this guidebook are applicable to all learners, particularly English learners and students with learning difficulties. We make the case that the strategies act as "language scaffolds" while English learners are developing English vocabulary and skills, and they act as "cognitive processing scaffolds" for students with learning difficulties who need extra support processing language and concepts and retaining and retrieving information.

WHO SHOULD READ THIS BOOK

We wrote this guidebook for middle and high school teachers who are looking for a practical, evidence-based approach to help English learners and students with certain learning difficulties to access the content reflected in state standards. We also wrote this book for school and district leaders who are looking for a sustainable schoolwide or districtwide practice that respects diversity and celebrates inclusion. The information about students with learning difficulties (chapter 2) and English learners (chapter 3) is meant to help general education teachers who want to effectively teach all diverse learners in their classrooms and to help special education teachers better understand dual status students.

Although the classroom examples in this guidebook are situated at the middle and high school levels, we believe the ideas are equally applicable to primary grades, and it is our hope that elementary school teachers will be able to adapt the strategies and examples to fit their students and context. Although the examples in this guidebook are from language arts, mathematics, science, and social science lessons, we know teachers of other subjects, such as art, music, and culinary arts, who have enthusiastically and effectively adapted in their classrooms the strategies we recommend. Throughout this book, we speak of a teacher in a general education classroom that includes English learners and students with learning difficulties; however, we recognize and encourage a more effective inclusion model in which the general education teacher *co-teaches* with a bilingual or special education teacher.

TEAM LEARNING AND SUSTAINING PRACTICES

This guidebook can be used best as a common resource by teams of teachers who share the same students. Although one teacher in a school can benefit from this book, using it alone would be like trying to paddle a one-person raft upstream for a long time — it would become extremely difficult to refine and sustain practice over time. When a team of teachers at a school uses the guidebook for a "book study" in a professional learning community context, it is like sharing the paddling and navigating of one large raft downstream. Also, a student needs to experience the same effective practices for many years to graduate from high school prepared for a meaningful career or postsecondary education. An educated adult is not the result of one teacher at one grade level but of a long process of high-quality teachers working as a K–12 team.

Just as many students "come alive" in social learning activities, many teachers also feel efficacy and energy when part of a team working together in a professional learning community and seeing beneficial results in the classroom. We recommend meeting in such teams at least twice a month to ensure a continuous sharing and learning process reflecting the key components of a professional learning community: shared leadership, collective creativity, shared values and vision, supportive conditions, and shared personal practice. As an alternative, or in addition, a teacher can join or create an online personal learning network (PLN) to chat and blog within an interest group and to access resources.[7]

The proposed approach in this guidebook combines the science of teaching — integrated, research-based strategies used very frequently with a defined purpose and understanding — and the art of teaching wherein teachers infuse their passion to teach with their professionalism to collegially and continually teach better and share their unique personalities and life experiences with their students. With long-range planning and support of school and district leaders, this approach can become part of the school culture, sustaining common core practices through professional learning communities and a balance of whole-school and individual accountability. Professional learning that is effective and sustains new practices is built on principles such as shared values and goals, collective responsibility for student achievement, self-directed reflection, consistent time and place to work as a team, and strong leadership that supports teamwork.[8]

THESE STRATEGIES ARE A HANDFUL

The general approach and strategies in this guidebook are intended to anchor, or at least connect to, a variety of other strategies and techniques found in others' books, articles, and professional development sessions that work best for a specific student or address the complexity of a learning situation in much greater depth. In choosing particular strategies to recommend in this guidebook, we used the following criteria:

» The strategies have been identified in the research and/or professional literature as effective for general education students, English learners, and students with various learning difficulties. (Appendix A provides a chart that cites the main sources of research we have found that support the strategies recommended in this guidebook.)

» The strategies are doable — they are relatively simple to learn to use, and they can be used daily, throughout the day, in any discipline.

» The strategies are interconnected — one strategy flows into or can be embedded in another strategy, so a teacher can interweave them throughout a lesson as a whole approach to teaching diverse learners who can all "get it," just in different ways.

Occasionally we offer examples involving one student who is an English learner or one who has a learning difficulty or one who has dual status. The names used are fictitious, except for Tony, who is an English learner with autism and language processing difficulties and appears in examples throughout the book. We hope this use of individual students helps to personalize what we say academically. And, of course, we also welcome teachers to think about one or more special students from their own classrooms while reading this guidebook.

ENDNOTES FOR INTRODUCTION

[1] Fisher, D., Roach, V., & Frey, N. (2002). Examining the general programmatic benefits of inclusive schools. *International Journal of Inclusive Education, 6*(1), 63–78. See p. 74.

[2] Chamot, A. U., & O'Malley, J. M. (1994). *The Calla handbook: Implementing the Cognitive Academic Language Learning Approach.* White Plains, NY: Addison Wesley Longman.

[3] Echevarría, J., Vogt, M., & Short, D. J. (2008). *Making content comprehensible for English learners: The SIOP© model* (3rd ed.). Boston: Allyn & Bacon.

[4] Sherris, A. (2008, September). Integrated content and language instruction. In *CALdigest.* Washington, DC: Center for Applied Linguistics. Retrieved from http://www.cal.org; another source is Ellis, R. (2003). *Task-based language learning and teaching.* Cary, NC: Oxford Applied Linguistics.

[5] Carr, J., Carroll, C., Cremer, S., Gale, M., Lagunoff, R., & Sexton, U. (2009). *Making mathematics accessible to English learners: A guidebook for teachers.* San Francisco: WestEd; Carr, J., Sexton, U., & Lagunoff, R. (2007). *Making science accessible to English learners: A guidebook for teachers.* San Francisco: WestEd.

[6] Silverman, L. K. (2002). *Upside-down brilliance: The visual-spatial learner.* Denver: DeLeon Publishing. Research by Linda Silverman on validating an assessment of visual-spatial learning style with students in grades 4–6 indicated that about 30 percent were predominantly visual-spatial and 30 percent had a slight preference. This information is accessible from http://www.gifteddevelopment.com/Visual_Spatial_Learner/vsl.htm

[7] The Educator's PLN — http://edupln.ning.com — is an example. Facebook can be used as a PLN. For information on Moodles, wikis, Twitter, blogs, Nings, and RSS feeds, see Huber, C. (2010). Professional learning 2.0. *Educational Leadership, 67*(8), 41–46.

[8] National Commission on Teaching and America's Future. (2011). Team up for 21st century teaching and learning. *ASCD Express, 6*(19). Retrieved from http://www.ascd.org/ascdexpress

CHAPTER 1

A Framework for Planning and Teaching Effective Lessons

> **It is not the content that limits students' learning; it is the manner in which the content is taught.**
>
> — Silvia DeRuvo

This chapter offers a framework for teachers to use in planning and implementing inquiry-based instruction that is effective for diverse learners and doable for all teachers. We begin with three principles of learning and motivation that apply to all learners. We also provide definitions of differentiated instruction and inclusive classrooms. Then we describe a useful framework for engaging and empowering students as they inquire about or explore lesson topics, and we offer tips on how to differentiate instruction within that framework — ways to tailor instruction to fit the diverse ways students learn.

PRINCIPLES OF LEARNING AND MOTIVATION

Many of the recommendations about effective teaching and learning in the research and expert literature are linked to three simple principles. These research-based principles about how people learn are the foundation of all of the ideas and strategies presented in this guidebook, as they can provide a useful guide for effective teaching and learning.[1]

Principle 1 — Recognize students' preconceptions. Students come to the classroom with preconceptions about how the world works. If their initial understanding is not engaged, they may fail to grasp the new concepts and information that are taught or they may learn the new material for purposes of a test but revert to their preconceptions outside the classroom.

For English learners and students with certain learning difficulties, the teacher needs to use evidence-based strategies to concretely and explicitly connect what these students already know with what they need to learn at the start of a lesson, and, at a later point, explicitly state and visually point out what were initial misconceptions that need to be discarded in light of new information, the target concepts all students were expected to learn.

Principle 2 — Organize facts into conceptual frameworks. To develop competence in an area of inquiry, students must (a) have a deep foundation of factual knowledge, (b) understand facts and ideas in the context of a conceptual framework, and (c) organize knowledge in ways that facilitate retrieval and application.

English learners and students with learning difficulties need to learn facts and ideas and be able to relate to and organize them conceptually. English learners especially need the vocabulary of the concepts and the function words that connect concepts. The teacher needs to scaffold learning for these students to build conceptual understanding and make connections among concepts in concrete ways as well as frequently check for understanding.

Principle 3 — Use metacognition to help students learn how to learn. A metacognitive approach to instruction can help students learn to take control of their own learning by defining learning goals and monitoring their progress in achieving them.

English learners and students with learning difficulties benefit from reflecting on their learning goals and progress. English learners, unlike native English speakers, benefit from applying a metacognitive approach to learning English, as well as to learning discipline-specific content. Students with learning difficulties benefit when they understand how they think and learn best and then apply those strategies, especially when a teacher is teaching in a way that is not differentiated for the ways those students learn best.[2] The artful teacher brings these principles to life for each student, recognizing a student's current level of knowledge and understanding and facilitating each student's growth as a self-directed learner. A respectful classroom climate is key to a teacher's success in being able to do this.[3] This climate is a clear goal in the inclusive classroom in which students with learning difficulties and physical disabilities fully participate in social learning with general education students. Often a visitor can step into a classroom and feel a distinct climate, whether of respect and caring, fear of ridicule, or boredom and detachment. A positive climate is established by teacher modeling and facilitation and is sustained by student practice.

When teachers nurture a safe learning community within their classrooms, students respect each other's ideas, are patient with one another, recognize there can be multiple perspectives and ways of learning, and recognize the value of individual contributions to group learning. With their anxiety lowered, students are physiologically more able to accept new challenges and grapple with new concepts and problems.[4] Because students with specific learning needs may feel a high level of anxiety about all the challenges they face, it is especially important for them to feel respected by the teacher and other students.

WHAT DIFFERENTIATED INSTRUCTION IS AND IS NOT

The principles outlined above engender a belief that all students in an academic program can learn core concepts and skills, they can do so when concepts are organized and connected, and they can learn metacognitive skills for constructing conceptual frameworks to become confident, independent learners. The framework we recommend in this guidebook also emphasizes that instruction should be differentiated and classrooms should be inclusive.

Differentiation is *not* teaching one way to all students (what has been called one size fits all). It is *not* planning and implementing an individualized education program (an IEP in special education) for each student. It is *not* "teaching everything in at least three different ways."[5] Differentiation means expecting all students to master the same core concepts (standards) and, to meet that expectation, using different materials/resources, different ways of learning, and different ways of showing what was learned.[6] The learning standards are always a constant, but all students may not take the same well-worn path to proficiency. Differentiation is sometimes called personalized instruction because the teacher knows each student personally — their learning preferences and needs, their interests and backgrounds — and finds opportunities to tailor evidence-based strategies to connect with specific students on a very personal level. In a general education classroom with 30 students, getting to know each student may start with a survey in the first meeting, tips from the special education or English Language Development/English as a Second Language (ELD/ESL) teacher for inclusion students, and having students practice social learning skills in small groups by discussing topics such as how each student learns best. When students recognize there are different ways of learning and respect diversity, they readily understand and accept that some students may be given different texts to read, notes with sentence frames, and so on.

WHAT AN INCLUSIVE CLASSROOM IS AND IS NOT

An inclusive classroom does not provide an *equal* educational experience for all students; it provides an *equitable* education for all students. Widespread interest in differentiating instruction reflects the understanding that students learn in different ways. Providing a high-quality, equitable education for all students means planning and using a diversity of strategies that fit a diversity of students so all students have the opportunity to learn successfully. Differentiated teacher-led instruction and inquiry-based learning provide equitable access to the curriculum and standards for all diverse learners. Here are some key points about what an effective inclusive classroom is and is not:[7]

» It is not simply placing students with physical, intellectual, and learning difficulties in general education-inclusive environments — often students with special learning needs become marginalized, "tune out," or display disruptive behaviors to cope with their frustration.

» It is not having a special education teaching assistant sit beside the students with learning difficulties, passively listening to teacher talk.

» It is guided by a well-defined collaborative and communicative plan that is deliberately designed to support all students.

» It is helping the general education teacher plan and implement lessons that include doable differentiation.

» It is best done by co-planning and co-teaching lessons — a content expert working together with another teacher who has expertise in differentiation for students with specific learning needs.

A FRAMEWORK FOR TEACHING DIVERSE LEARNERS

For a practical and effective framework for teaching diverse learners in any core discipline, we have chosen the 5 Es model, which Roger W. Bybee proposed more than a decade ago for inquiry-based learning in science.[8] The 5 Es framework represents a recursive cycle of cognitive stages in inquiry-based learning: *engage, explore, explain, elaborate,* and *evaluate.* As the arrows in Figure 1.1 denote, the stages are not necessarily linear; there may well be back-and-forth progression between stages, especially between *explore* and *explain* and between *explain* and *elaborate.* The *evaluate* stage crosses into the other four as students frequently reflect on what they do and do not know and the teacher frequently checks students' understanding and adjusts instruction accordingly. Typically, not all five stages would be experienced in a single 50-minute lesson, but all five would certainly be embedded in a unit lesson lasting several days or longer. The 5 Es framework is useful as a guide — not a rigid template — for lesson planning, particularly when the lesson emphasizes

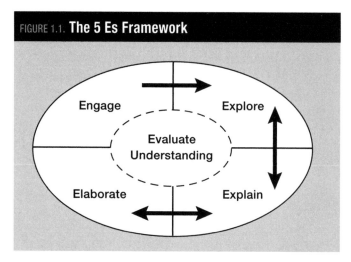

FIGURE 1.1. **The 5 Es Framework**

Source: Carr, J., Sexton, U., & Lagunoff, R. (2007). *Making science accessible to English learners: A guidebook for teachers.* San Francisco: WestEd.

inquiry-based, small-group instruction.[9] The 5 Es approach capitalizes on hands-on activities, students' curiosity, and academic discussion among students. It should be a key part of all students' education, explicitly connected to target concepts and content standards and used in conjunction with other methods, including direct instruction.

Guided by this framework, the teacher begins the lesson by engaging students in what they are about to learn and making connections to what they already know (Principle 1 of learning and motivation). The teacher then guides students as they explore a topic, use new information to explain it, and elaborate or expand conceptual thinking (Principle 2) while evaluating the learning process throughout the lesson (Principle 3). The 5 Es framework is similar to a "3+1 phase model" for teaching mathematics that has been promoted by the National Council of Teachers of Mathematics;[10] however, the 5 Es has an explicit stage called *elaborate* in which students make inferences, predictions, and generalizations and apply concepts and skills to new situations. The *explore, explain,* and *elaborate* stages fit the new Common Core standards quite well; for example, students are expected to explore different ideas collaboratively, explain how a main idea is supported by certain evidence or details, and elaborate on a theme by comparing and contrasting different sources.

We see the 5 Es as a flexible cycle of stages that a teacher can use as a framework when planning a multiday lesson that will engage all students in active, hands-on learning and in using academic language in meaningful ways. This approach works for all students, but especially well for English learners and students with learning difficulties. In this chapter, we explicate each of the 5 Es, suggest how to balance teacher-led and student-led instruction within the framework, and explain the relevance for English learners and students with learning difficulties. Later, in chapters 4 and 5, we explain specific strategies that can be embedded within the 5 Es framework to tailor or differentiate instruction for students with special learning needs.

Engage

The teacher starts the learning process by involving students in making connections between their past and present learning experiences. This stage is meant to create interest, generate curiosity, and raise questions and problems, helping students engage in their own learning process while facilitating opportunities for the teacher to identify students' preconceptions. At this time some misconceptions may surface, and they are acknowledged along with other brainstorming ideas. This alerts the teacher to ensure that the lesson explicitly addresses these misconceptions at the proper time, when the teacher will clearly identify why some ideas are valid and some are not.

> **In my classroom**[11] ... I begin my lesson plan with an intriguing idea, image, or question to engage students. I pose questions about what my students already know, make conjectures about how to solve a problem, and encourage students to pose questions about what they want to learn. This alerts me to what students already know, their misconceptions, and areas of potential confusion. I let students know at the start of each lesson what our content and language objectives are so that students understand the purpose of the activity.
>
> This way of beginning helps me personalize the lesson and thereby engage diverse students by planning statements or questions that connect to certain students' culture, native language, other background factors (e.g., neighborhood the student lives in), or personal interests (e.g., the student who is hooked on all things about airplanes). To do this, I need to know each student personally, and the first step is an "About Me" activity on the first day of class that gives students an opportunity to tell about themselves.
>
> For a student with a learning difficulty such as attention-deficit/hyperactivity disability (ADHD) or autism spectrum disorder (ASD), I may make explicit how the new lesson/content is relevant to the student's interests/experiences and connected to prior knowledge. To do this, I may use video clips, relevant discussion, or challenges to prove or disprove a statement or investigate the answer to a provocative question.[12] Visual supports may be necessary for English learners and for making the connections very explicit for students with learning difficulties.
>
> As part of engaging students, I make explicit the content and language objectives that are the focus of the lesson. I present these objectives to students orally and in writing to make clear how the planned discussions and activities will address course standards and English language standards. When I make learning objectives explicit, it helps all students focus on the target from the start of the lesson, and it sets the basis for students to reflect on how well they achieved the objectives at the end of the lesson.

Explore

The teacher guides students as they investigate or perform an experiment about a phenomenon and arrive at a common understanding of certain concepts, processes, and skills. The teacher designs activities that encourage students to construct new knowledge or skills, propose preliminary predictions and hypotheses, puzzle through problems, and try alternatives to answer a question.

In my classroom ... I do not explain to students the concepts I want them to eventually know. Instead, I expect them to think critically about the concepts by experimenting, investigating, observing, classifying, communicating, predicting, and interpreting. This active engagement arouses curiosity and leads students to discover new ideas, confirm prior assumptions, and perhaps challenge their thinking.

English learners might not be able to explore a topic independently and may need language support that can be provided by working in a small group. Students with learning difficulties might be able to explore a topic independently but may have difficulty with organization or processing information and may benefit from peers to help them keep on track or organize new information. Both types of students need directions for a task to be written in simple language, and both may need to see models of a finished product, not just stated orally by the teacher; the student with learning difficulties may need directions expanded into a series of ministeps, whereas other students may be able to conduct an exploration guided by major steps.

To participate in small-group explorations, English learners may need discussion sentence starters to scaffold their comments, and students with learning difficulties may need peers to model how to actively listen and respectfully speak in a small group.

Explain

The teacher guides students as they demonstrate or explain their conceptual understanding, process skills, or behaviors. They debate alternative explanations and contrast new facts with prior misconceptions. As appropriate, the teacher directs students' attention to aspects of their earlier experiences from the *engage* and *explore* stages. Students organize information into evidence-based statements, using the academic language of the discipline.

As students construct meaning from their explorations and text, the teacher may deem it necessary to intervene — by providing further evidence, raw data, or other resources or interactions — so as to model closer examination of evidence to correct misconceptions. By providing a safe environment in which to express ideas, the teacher allows students to consider alternative interpretations and test new ideas while continuing to build understanding based on empirical and quantitative evidence. This question-and-answer session might occur after small-group discussion to lower student anxiety by stating the group's idea instead of one's own idea.

In my classroom ... I guide students' thinking by using questioning and by facilitating peer discussions to arrive at explanations. I give students time to think, and I facilitate student-student discussions to correct misconceptions. It is a time to question and justify answers. Students do not just pose questions and I answer, nor do they simply give answers and I decide what is right or wrong.

I offer discussion sentence starters on the wall as a reference for English learners and students with learning difficulties to use and discuss their ideas and have them listen to and offer ideas in a pair or trio to provide a low anxiety context, and then I ask for group ideas during a whole-class discussion.

Elaborate

The teacher monitors activities and facilitates discussions that challenge and extend students' conceptual understanding and skills. Students apply what they learned to new experiences to develop, extend, connect, and deepen their understanding.

> **In my classroom ...** I help students compare, contrast, combine, synthesize, generalize, and make inferences by introducing a somewhat different context from what they just experienced, a context that is much less cognitively demanding so they understand the skill and then apply it to the cognitively demanding topic of my lesson. I want students to apply new knowledge, make connections, and extend ideas, and I am shifting from me deciding what graphic organizer best suits the context to student groups making that decision.

Evaluate Understanding

The teacher evaluates students' progress and students assess themselves throughout the other stages. Feedback may come from checking for understanding (e.g., with hand gestures, whiteboards), quizzes, student discussions, or journals, to name a few techniques. The teacher uses the feedback to reflect on the effectiveness of the lesson, making midcourse adjustments as indicated to better fit the needs and interests of students. The students use the feedback to reflect on what they understand and what they still need to learn or want to know next.

> **In my classroom ...** I test more than factual knowledge; I challenge students to construct ideas and explanations during an assessment. I want students to construct knowledge and build skills during instruction, and I want assessments to reflect my objectives and the content standards. I check for understanding in a variety of ways, such as taking notes while I monitor small groups, asking probing questions of certain students, and checking their journal entries as their "ticket out" of my classroom at the end of the lesson.

Between presenting chunks of information during teacher-directed instruction, and while monitoring group work, the teacher should check in a variety of ways for students' understanding of the target content and learning strategies. Often, effective teachers focus on how students arrived at their answers before focusing on whether their answers are correct. This emphasizes the importance of the strategy used to get an answer as well as the answer itself.

Checking for understanding informs teachers of what and how their students are learning during the lesson, and making adjustments can result in greater achievement for all students.[13] Checking for understanding can unearth misconceptions before or at the start of direct instruction. This allows the teacher to identify key vocabulary words and concepts that will likely need more explicit teaching than anticipated and to know which students will need this more intensive instruction. The teacher is aware that misconceptions may need to be addressed through small-group tasks involving experimentation or inquiry. Misconceptions that are identified midway through a lesson may lead the teacher to go back to an earlier stage and adjust the inquiry task.

Research indicates that learning improves for the whole class and the achievement gap narrows when the teacher uses techniques to get feedback about what each student does or does not understand during direct instruction and group work and immediately makes appropriate adjustments in instruction.[14] Bloom reported that the average student in a group that learned a math unit with checking for understanding (and lesson adjustment) outperformed 84 percent of a group of students who received direct instruction with no checking for understanding and lesson adjustments.[15] Also, the range of test scores was much narrower for the "checking for understanding" group. So it appears that the time taken to frequently check for understanding and consider ways to adjust the lesson to fit struggling students is well worth the impact on whole-class learning.

Calling on individual students is a way for the teacher to collect feedback from a few students at a time. Alternative ways to check for understanding can provide a broader range of information and encourage all students to respond:

» Students use whiteboards to write and display short answers.

» Students signal agreement/disagreement/confusion with a point of view, solution, or approach, using colored cards or hand gestures (e.g., thumbs up/down/sideways).

» The teacher randomly draws a stick with a student's name on it; after the student answers, the rest of the class uses signals (see above) to agree or disagree.

» Students work in teams to respond. For example, teams contribute to a collective class solution to a problem; or partners talk with one another in English or their primary language before reporting to the class in English.

» Students use an approach called "Ticket Out," in which they record on a piece of paper or in their journal a follow-up question or one idea that they learned, that was interesting, or that needs clarification. The teacher reviews the student feedback, which then informs the teacher's decisions about the next day's lesson. Student pairs, such as a novice English learner with a more proficient English speaker, might record an idea while others do so individually.

When checking for understanding by asking a question of the whole class, the teacher should wait at least five seconds so that all students have ample opportunity to process the question and think about an answer (three to seven seconds or more, depending on the difficulty of the question). The teacher may acknowledge early hand raisers with a nod while still waiting to give everyone time to think of an answer. This wait time allows English learners and students with learning difficulties to decipher the question, think, and formulate an answer. It also encourages more students to respond. To resist the urge to keep the lesson pace moving rapidly, the teacher may use a technique such as counting silently or pacing the floor one step per second. When the teacher calls on a student, walking close to the student may lessen the student's anxiety about speaking aloud in front of many peers. And it can be particularly helpful for English learners and students with learning difficulties to hear other students rephrase information when responding, as this provides additional opportunities to learn vocabulary and comprehend important ideas.

While students are discussing their ideas during group work, the teacher should walk around and listen to students, particularly those who may be struggling to comprehend the content or express their thoughts, such as English learners and students with learning difficulties. If a student in the group is unable to assist the struggling student, the teacher may softly provide guidance and, when the group work is planned to take a long time, provide small-group instruction for the students who are struggling. If many groups are having difficulty with the task, the teacher should stop them and adjust instruction.

The role of the teacher in the 5 Es cycle is multifaceted. As a facilitator, the teacher nurtures creative thinking, problem solving, interaction, communication, and discovery. As a model, the teacher initiates thinking processes, inspires positive attitudes toward learning, motivates, and demonstrates skill-building techniques. Finally, as a guide, the teacher helps to bridge language gaps and foster individuality, collaboration, and personal growth. The teacher flows in and out of these various roles within each lesson, both when planned and as opportunities arise.

For a more detailed description of student and teacher roles during 5 Es instruction within the context of a science lesson, see Figure 1.2.

FIGURE 1.2. **The 5 Es Instructional Framework in Science**

Purpose	Teacher Role	Student Role
Engage		
To initiate the lesson. An engagement activity connects past and present learning experiences, anticipates new ideas, and organizes students' thinking toward standards and outcomes.	» create interest » generate curiosity » raise questions and problems » elicit responses that uncover students' current knowledge about the concept/topic	» ask questions such as "Why did this happen?" "What do I already know about this?" "What can I find out about this?" "How can this problem be solved?" » show interest in the topic
Explore		
To provide students with a common base of experiences within which current concepts, processes, and skills are identified and developed.	» guide students to work together without direct instruction » observe and listen to students as they interact » ask probing questions to redirect students' investigations as needed » provide time for students to puzzle through problems » act as a consultant for students	» think creatively within the limits of the activity » generate and test predictions and hypotheses » form new predictions and hypotheses » try alternatives to solve a problem and discuss them » record observations and ideas » suspend judgment » test ideas

FIGURE 1.2. **The 5 Es Instructional Framework in Science (continued)**

Purpose	Teacher Role	Student Role
Explain		
To focus students on a particular aspect of their prior-stage experiences. This stage provides opportunities for students to demonstrate their conceptual understanding and process skills. This stage may be an opportunity to introduce a concept, process, or skill.	» formally provide definitions, explanations, and new vocabulary » use students' previous experiences as the basis for explaining concepts » guide students to explain concepts and definitions in their own words » ask for justification (evidence) and clarification from students	» explain possible solutions or answers to other students » listen critically to and respectfully question other students' explanations » listen and try to comprehend explanations offered by the teacher » refer to previous activities
Elaborate		
To challenge and extend students' conceptual understanding and skills. Through new experiences, students develop deeper and broader understanding, more information, and adequate skills.	» expect students to use learned academic language, concepts, and skills in a new context » remind students of alternative explanations » refer students to alternative explanations	» apply new labels, definitions, explanations, and skills in new but related situations » use previous information to ask questions, propose solutions, make decisions, and design experiments » draw reasonable conclusions from evidence » record observations or explanations
Evaluate		
To encourage students to assess their understanding and abilities and to provide opportunities for teachers to evaluate student progress.	» observe students as they apply new concepts and skills » assess students' knowledge or skills » ask students to assess their learning and group process skills » ask open-ended questions such as "What evidence do you have?" "What do you know about the problem?"	» check for understanding among peers » answer open-ended questions by using observations, evidence, and previously accepted explanations » demonstrate an understanding of the concept or skill » evaluate own progress » ask related questions that would encourage future investigations

Source: R.W. Bybee (1997). *Achieving scientific inquiry: From purposes to practices.* Portsmouth, NH: Heinemann. Adapted with permission.

TWO TYPES OF INSTRUCTION WITHIN THE FRAMEWORK

Two types of instruction occur within each stage of the five Es framework – teacher-led and student-led instruction, as illustrated in Figure 1.3 where a one-directional arrow signifies moving from teacher-led to student-led instruction and a two-directional arrow signifies a back-and-forth cycle. Figure 1.3 is an elaboration of Figure 1.1. The teacher may have planned to deliver instruction in chunks in which each chunk is followed by a reinforcing small-group activity while the teacher checks for understanding. If noticing that some groups are struggling too much, the teacher may stop those or all groups and reteach to clarify key concepts or processes.

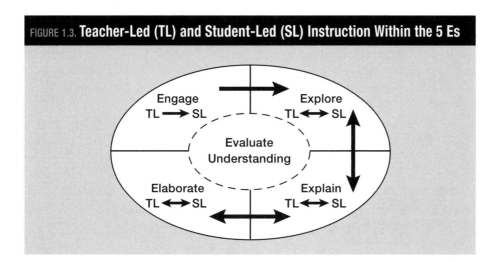

FIGURE 1.3. **Teacher-Led (TL) and Student-Led (SL) Instruction Within the 5 Es**

We focus on a certain kind of student-led instruction that involves inquiry-based learning within small groups because it can be highly effective for English learners and students with learning difficulties when the teacher carefully prepares task directions that are easily understood and prepares students regarding the requisite academic and social skills to successfully complete the group task. A teacher may need to monitor particular students closely and intervene when a student is not behaving appropriately. Establishing and using consistent routines will diminish interruptions and inappropriate behaviors.

It should be obvious that the teacher does *not* do all of the talking throughout the 5 Es. Too much teacher talk tends to center students' attention on the teacher as the source of all knowledge and greatly limits "student talk" to interaction with the teacher rather than peers. This kind of instruction takes away opportunities for English learners to practice using new academic language in meaningful social learning situations and takes away opportunities for students with specific learning needs to hear from peers and talk to peers in the comfort of a small group. Many students may be confused about directions and be too shy to ask for clarity or may find it extremely difficult to maintain attention and so fail to independently complete a task. They may sit and seemingly be doing nothing, appearing to the teacher that they are disinterested and defiantly choosing not to engage in the task. But if placed in pairs or triads of supportive peers, often these students can complete the task successfully.

The teacher who knows his or her students with specific learning needs knows that they can reach language or cognitive overload when the teacher talks for a long time. This teacher balances teacher-led instruction with student-led instruction. Effective student-led instruction and inquiry require that students participate in small groups, ideally pairs or triads, to complete a meaningful task such as an experiment, math problem, history task, or compare and contrast assignment. This balancing of teacher-led and student-led discussions and activities is depicted in Figure 1.3.

Teacher-Led Instruction

Teacher-led instruction, even though teacher-centered, can play a key role in classrooms that address the needs of diverse students, including English learners and students with specific learning needs. Teacher-led instruction is sometimes informally called teacher talk. The teacher addresses the whole class, and individual students respond to the teacher; most interactions are teacher-student. The teacher uses brief periods of oral instruction supported by visuals to initiate concept development, demonstrate a new skill to the whole class, and model expected student behaviors for small-group work. Visuals that support teacher talk can be pictures, illustrations, relevant objects, graphic organizers, models, demonstrations, and video clips. Teacher-directed instruction gives students access to the information they need to process and manipulate ideas, clarify concepts, and build the connections among concepts that lead to greater understanding of content subject matter.

English learners and students with learning difficulties especially need teachers to provide comprehensible input, using language and speech students can understand. Providing comprehensible input does not mean "dumbed down"; it does mean avoiding unknown idioms and highly complex sentences, emphasizing key words, and pausing frequently. The teacher plans the statements and questions to say, supported by visuals, to engage students at the beginning of a new lesson to connect prior knowledge to the concepts to be learned in this lesson. Then the teacher moves into stating what all students will learn (or be able to do), identifies key words or terms that are appropriate to frontload the lesson, and guides students to create informal definitions, which will be refined as formal definitions at a later time. The teacher may "think aloud" to model for students how a scientist ponders a phenomenon, how a mathematician goes about selecting and using a strategy to solve a problem, or how a literary critic comes to understand the meaning of a poem or theme of a story. The teacher interweaves information being presented with questions (e.g., "What do you think will happen if ...?") to spur student thinking or check for understanding. The teacher does not simply stand and present information for a long time as if students are empty vessels being filled with facts; the presentation is based on an understanding that humans construct new knowledge and interact with their preconceptions.

We encourage teachers to refrain from being the sole source of correct information in the room. Even when leading the class in direct instruction, it often can be helpful to refrain from indicating the correct (or incorrect) answer to a question and instead require students to interact and agree on a correct answer. This shifts the source of expertise from the teacher to the students, who must then become experts and critical thinkers. When a student asks a question, the teacher often should encourage other students to respond. When a student gives an answer, quick techniques such as thumbs up/down can be used to poll the whole class on whether an answer is correct, appropriate, or applicable. The teacher can then facilitate respectful discussion among students that includes supporting evidence and reasoning. This requires all students to listen intently to a student's answer and evaluate its correctness. Through thoughtful questioning techniques, the teacher can facilitate and probe to encourage critical thinking, respond to student questions with meaningful questions that engage the students in further dialogue with each other, and promote the revision or review of their interpretations based on the evidence at hand.

For many students with specific learning needs, a middle or high school teacher should talk no more than 10 minutes (less time for lower grades) to orally give students information about a concept or skill, interspersed with questions to guide their thinking and promote active listening. WestEd researcher Silvia DeRuvo suggests a 10:2 rule — no more than 10 minutes of teacher talk followed by 2 minutes of checking for understanding or response.[16] The teacher should wait about 7 seconds (it could be shorter or longer for some students) between asking a question and accepting student answers to give students with specific learning needs enough time to process the question, consider an answer, and formulate an answer in words.[17]

Applications of Teacher-Led Instruction for Students with Specific Learning Needs

Teacher modeling is an important support for students with specific learning needs. These students need to preview completed projects such as writing assignments and the rubrics that specify performance expectations and make the assessments transparent to students; some English learners may never have had formal schooling or participated in similar tasks in their former countries. Similarly, before students engage in group work, the teacher needs to model expected discourse and social behaviors and procedures.

When speaking to students, the teacher can target the listening abilities of English learners and students with language reception/processing difficulties in terms of enunciation, speed, intonation, and use of vocabulary, idioms, and contractions. For example, English learners at novice levels require simple subject-verb-object sentences, free of idioms and colloquial expressions. (It can be surprising how many expressions such as "no way" and "make up your mind" and "come up with your answer" pepper typical classroom instruction, to the befuddlement of English learners.) The student with autism spectrum disorder may misinterpret an idiom by taking it quite literally ("it's raining cats and dogs").

When an English learner responds in a manner that moves the discussion forward, the teacher may use rephrasing to clarify the idea for all students and model desired academic discourse. For example, if an English learner says, "*equal square* is a curve," the teacher might respond, "Yes, the graph of *equals squared* is a parabola [drawing or pointing to it], a line that curves." The rephrasing is most helpful to the English learner if it is just a level above what the student produced independently. The student may choose to repeat the teacher's rephrased statement, but should not be asked to do so. Rephrasing helps all students gradually develop more sophisticated academic discourse skills. This can happen in a safe, respectful environment when students feel comfortable with their classmates and recognize the importance of everyone's contributions to group learning.

Much more can be said about effective teacher-led instruction, but we assume teachers have had ample professional development on this pedagogical approach for teaching most students in the classroom, though not necessarily on how to build in differentiation for English learners and students with learning difficulties so that all students can learn successfully. The main emphasis we hope to convey here is the importance of *blending oral instruction with visual aids*; planning how to *build in small, explicit steps toward a complex concept or relationship among concepts*; and crafting *word choice and emphasis, sentence complexity, and strategic pauses at the level of comprehensible input* for the most challenged students.[18]

These suggestions can be recast as tips that give students with specific learning needs equitable access to the curriculum and learning standards:

» Support oral instruction with visuals (e.g., gestures, pictures, writing or pointing to key words on poster paper, filling in part of a graphic organizer).

» Avoid idioms that all students do not know, complex sentences, and going off on a tangent.

» Emphasize key words orally and visually and check for understanding of words some English learners may not yet know (e.g., the word *conversely* in science signals a nonexample of a key concept).

» Build small chunks, or ministeps, toward a complex idea.

» Give students thinking time to process each idea using the 10:2 rule.

» Wait 5–7 seconds after posing a question before taking an answer. If a student starts to answer and pauses, be patient and let the student finish communicating the thought. Jumping in to "help" or "save" the student only interrupts the student's thinking and devalues thinking time.

Student-Led Instruction

Student-led instruction in which relatively high- and low-performing readers are paired, taking turns as tutor and tutee, is very effective for English learners and students with learning difficulties, particularly for students in the primary grades working on reading word attack and fluency skills, and for students in upper elementary grades working on reading comprehension. Students practice reading skills while practicing oral language skills with peers in English. An inclusive classroom in a school that implements the Response to Intervention (RTI) model provides a natural setting to implement student-led instruction because an inclusive classroom contains a diversity of students and RTI focuses on targeted, research-based interventions in the general education classroom.[19]

Meaningful group work is typically the basis for student-led instruction, also called peer-assisted instruction. This is at the heart of social learning in the classroom. Moreover, the English language arts Common Core standards that most states have adopted or adapted directly address collaborative learning skills (see Appendix B). As mentioned earlier, before students begin complex group activities, the teacher may need to model the expected group learning behaviors and establish rules of conduct. Students teach each other and learn together while the teacher monitors, guides, and models as necessary. In cooperative learning, one type of student-led instruction, each student in a group has a different role and/or subtask. Klingner suggests altering the structure so that students take turns leading a discussion and use a strategy to complete a subtask, and all students complete their own learning logs.[20]

Social learning can be defined as a group of students discussing ideas and helping each other to learn. It is an integral part of student-led instruction and can be effective for English learners and for students with learning difficulties when the teacher models target language and discussion expectations, provides visual language supports, and monitors and guides students as they work collaboratively in small groups.[21] Social learning is effective because it promotes a rich environment for the use of academic language, such as problem-solving discussions that require use of a discipline's academic terminology. Students are expected to practice purposeful listening and speaking skills. As they work in small groups, English learners and students with learning difficulties hear their peers rephrase what the teacher has said and discuss their ideas, preferably with the support of visuals and hands-on activities.[22]

During small-group activities, the teacher monitors students' academic, social, and English language learning as they propose and try alternative problem-solving strategies and explain their conceptual thinking through speaking and writing. In a supportive classroom, English learners and students with learning difficulties benefit from a variety of such collaborations, which offer repeated opportunities to participate in discourse that builds their knowledge.[23] The language usage with peers especially helps English learners. The rephrasing of key concepts with peers especially helps students with learning difficulties.

To elaborate on the recommendations, we present a list of best instructional practices for diverse learners to participate in small-group discussions and work in inclusive classrooms:[24]

» Provide a rich, meaning-centered context for students to use language, with many visual representations, hands-on activities, and language supports.

» Provide ample opportunities for high-quality interaction between English learners and native English speakers that encourage English learners to share their knowledge and experiences, hear other students rephrase what the teacher said, and apply new language.

» Use high-frequency vocabulary that students know and gradually introduce more academic vocabulary as they progress in the lesson and their language skills.

» Integrate listening, speaking, reading, and writing skills across instruction and assist English learners and certain students with learning difficulties to build a bridge between oral and written language.

Student-led instruction reinforces ideas through discussion with peers and through practice using new vocabulary, and it lowers anxiety by giving students opportunities to speak to just one or a few peers before offering the group's agreed-upon answer during whole-class discussion. For small groups to work together well and stay on task, the teacher must model and guide students in the requisite social skills. Affixing placards with discussion sentence starters (e.g., "I agree with you because ..." "I have a different idea; it is ...") can help English learners, students with language production difficulties, and students with other learning difficulties to verbalize and organize their ideas. Chapter 4 presents a set of discussion starters.

GROUP SIZE MATTERS

The optimum group size depends on the task, the students, and the class context. A group size of four is appropriate for cooperative learning tasks, a type of collaborative learning in which each group member has an assigned role (e.g., facilitator, timekeeper, recorder) or subtask and there is both group and individual accountability.[25] In collaborative tasks that are less structured, with informal or no individual roles, a group size of three or four might still be effective, but the teacher should observe whether any individual members are less involved or completely marginalized, particularly students with specific learning needs. For collaborative tasks such as a one- or two-minute discussion/sharing of ideas, we recommend pairs or triads because in larger groups, some students will not get time to speak.[26] Longer discussions or tasks could involve trios, increasing the chance of more diverse ideas being offered and discussed. A teacher might start the year using pairs and shift to trios when students have attained the requisite social learning skills.[27]

GROUP COMPOSITION MATTERS

For the optimum mix of abilities in a group, generally we recommend that teachers select group members rather than letting students self-select. Members should not have widely disparate abilities (e.g., not the highest-ability paired with lowest-ability student), and in groups of three or more, higher-achieving students should not be the majority because they may unintentionally marginalize the student who needs a slower pace or more peer support. A teacher should conscientiously change group membership based on current formative assessments of students' needs, achievement, and being able to work well and comfortably with particular students.[28]

Grouping decisions should serve the teacher's strategic goals, one of which is to provide a risk-free, comfortable setting for each student to learn and express ideas. A teacher might plan alternative tasks such as writing a poem, short story, or play about a common theme and allow students to choose a group according to interest. The teacher might change group membership according to the task and academic and social goals and just to mix things up from time to time. Grouping English learners by primary language allows the students in the group to use their common native language or combine it with English to comfortably discuss ideas or create a product and then switch to English when sharing ideas with the whole class. When a goal is for students to practice using academic English with peers, the teacher should distribute English learners with a common native language (e.g., Spanish) into different groups.

Sometimes it is appropriate to group English learners so they interact with students at the same or adjacent English language levels and other times to interact with students who are more proficient in English to serve as language models. When mixing language levels, we recommend placing the English learner who is at a low-proficiency level with an English learner who is just one or two levels higher, not with an English learner at the highest level, so the higher-level student does serve as an English model but also is challenged to practice receptive and expressive skills in English. Generally speaking, students with the same or similar learning difficulties should not be grouped together, depending upon their strengths and needs. Some teachers report that separating these students benefits both students with special needs (e.g., weaknesses in learning, using oral language to express ideas, social skills) and students who do not have special needs.

For a student with exceptionally high intellect ("gifted"), the teacher may sometimes want to allow that student to work alone or work on elaboration tasks with similar students, as the student may prefer such opportunities over being grouped with students who are at a lower ability level. Teachers should keep inclusion in mind and be aware that for the students with learning difficulties, just being in the same classroom is not sufficient; it is the meaningful interaction with diverse peers that is essential for all students to learn.

Figure 1.4 narrates a teacher's grouping decisions for English learners.

FIGURE 1.4. Grouping by Language or Student Choice

This scenario, which shows the advantages of grouping students by their primary language, is from the teacher of a high school mathematics classroom with 35 students, representing six languages (English, Spanish, Vietnamese, Mandarin, Tagalog, and Russian).[29]

Grouping. Often I plan flexible student groupings for mathematics tasks, mixing students by primary language, English literacy, and/or mathematics literacy. Other times I allow students to select their own groups, and they usually select friends who speak their language. Today, I allow students to self-select, and most do so by their primary language.

Modeling. I start by posing an authentic context to the class. I give directions to be sure students understand the expectations of the task and model some of the discourse I expect of students involved in this task. I point to sentence starters on the wall that scaffold English learners to articulate their thoughts (e.g., "I agree with ___ that …"; "What if we …"; "I think that …").

Group learning. Then student groups talk about and complete their tasks. Discussions within the self-selected groups of English learners are typically a mix of English and primary language, depending on the group members' needs and comfort levels. For example, a group of English learners mixes Spanish and English during their discussion, with the more advanced English learners rephrasing certain ideas in Spanish for a very limited English learner who is showing difficulty understanding the English. I walk around to answer questions and ensure that they are all learning successfully. Later, when we have the full-class discussion in English, the most-limited-English proficient learners will have a good idea of what is being said because it was first discussed within the homogeneous language group.

The advantage to having students use their language of choice for peer-assisted learning and problem solving is that the focus stays on the content. Students are not inhibited by their varying abilities to communicate in English, so they can really understand the concepts in the day's activity. However, many times I form heterogeneous groups by mixing more proficient and limited English learners with different primary languages so students must use only English to convey their ideas and must practice using new academic vocabulary, and the more proficient English learners and native English speakers are models for the limited English learners.

Discussing. Next, I lead a whole-class discussion in English about what they did and said. I write students' answers as English sentences, projected so that they all can see.

The more proficient the English learner, the more elaborate I expect his or her comments to be. I do not ask dumbed-down questions, but I do adjust questions to be comprehensible for my English learners. When they finish responding, I selectively rephrase answers to model mathematics discourse and incorporate key vocabulary. This mathematical rephrasing benefits all students in the class.

Some basic steps prepare students to work effectively in teams or small groups and ensure that English learners will be able to participate and learn. To design effective cooperative and collaborative activities, the teacher makes sure that an activity is cognitively challenging for everyone while varying the language demands students must meet in order to participate and contribute. The activity is also structured to be "group worthy," meaning that it necessitates collaboration and discussion.[30]

By setting clear directions and expectations for group work, the teacher sets the best conditions for students to focus on learning. In classrooms with English learners and students with learning difficulties, directions should be written as well as oral. When the teacher writes the directions before giving them orally, it provides an opportunity to check that they are clear.

Sometimes students working in groups misbehave or become passive because they do not understand the concepts or the task instructions. To remedy this, the teacher may need to initiate group work by modeling expected behaviors and gradually shifting ownership of the group learning process to the students. Assigning roles is one way to help groups manage their interactions and structure successful participation for everyone. For example, a novice English learner in a group could participate as the illustrator of key concepts, and the more English proficient students could be assigned to act as facilitator, writer, or reporter. As they gain more experience and success, students can choose their own roles or collaborate more interdependently. Regardless of how groups are structured, teachers should set the expectation and provide the opportunity for all students to learn and accomplish the goal of the lesson.

Some students learn better in small groups than they do individually. Small-group talk gives English learners a chance for language repetition and practice, so differentiation also means planning for collaborative and cooperative learning activities. The focus of differentiation is to be aware of all the ways students are different from one another and to plan to teach in ways that capitalize on those differences.

Chapters 2 and 3 provide basic information about students with certain learning difficulties and English learners as a step in the direction of knowing individual students, which enables teachers to personalize instruction and form small groups within the 5 Es framework. Chapters 4 and 5 identify and describe instructional strategies that can be used within the 5 Es framework for building students' academic language and accessing rigorous content and learning standards.

ENDNOTES FOR CHAPTER 1

[1] National Research Council. (1999). *How people learn: Bridging research and practice.* Washington, DC: National Academies Press; National Research Council. (2005). *How students learn: History, mathematics, and science in the classroom.* Washington, DC: National Academies Press.

[2] Garner, B. K. (2007). *Getting to "got it!" Helping struggling students learn how to learn.* Alexandria, VA: Association for Supervision and Curriculum Development. This book describes what a clinician discovered about how "failing and frustrated" students learned, and what these students did to use their individual strengths to compensate when the teacher was not addressing learning differences in the classroom.

[3] Chapin, S., & O'Connor, C. (2007). Academically productive talk: Supporting students' learning in mathematics. In W. G. Martin, M. E. Strutchens, & P. C. Elliott (Eds.), *The learning of mathematics: Sixty-ninth yearbook* (pp. 113–128). Reston,

VA: National Council of Teachers of Mathematics; Boaler, J., & Humphreys, C. (2005). *Connecting mathematical ideas: Middle school video cases to support teaching and learning.* Portsmouth, NH: Heinemann.

[4] Weiss, R. P. (2000, July). Brain-based learning: The wave of the brain. *Training & Development,* 20–24. Retrieved from http://www.dushkin.com/text-data/articles/32638/body.pdf

[5] Carolan, J., & Guinn, A. (2007). Differentiation: Lessons from master teachers. *Educational Leadership, 64*(5), 44–47.

[6] Cole, R. W. (Ed.). (1995). *Educating everybody's children: Diverse teaching strategies for diverse learners.* Alexandria, VA: Association for Supervision and Curriculum Development; Cole, R. W. (Ed.). (2001). *More strategies for educating everybody's children.* Alexandria, VA: Association for Supervision and Curriculum Development; Gregory, G., & Chapman, C. (2001). *Differentiated instructional strategies: One size doesn't fit all.* Thousand Oaks, CA: Corwin Press; Silver, H. F., Strong, R. W., & Perini, M. J. (2000). *So each may learn.* Alexandria, VA: Association for Supervision and Curriculum Development; Tomlinson, C. A. (1999). *The differentiated classroom: Responding to the needs of all students.* Alexandria, VA: Association for Supervision and Curriculum Development; Tomlinson, C. A., & McTighe, J. (2006). *Integrating and differentiating instruction: Understanding by design.* Alexandria, VA: Association for Supervision and Curriculum Development.

[7] Hawkins, B. (2005). Mathematics education for second language students in the mainstream classroom. In P. A. Richard-Amato & M. A. Snow (Eds.), *Academic success for English language learners* (pp. 337–397). White Plains, NY: Pearson Education.

[8] Bybee, R. W. (1997). *Achieving scientific literacy: From purposes to practices.* Portsmouth, NH: Heinemann.

[9] Duran, E., Duran, L., Haney, J., & Scheuermann, A. (2011, March). A learning cycle for all students. *The Science Teacher, 78*(3), 56–60.

[10] Martin, T. S. (Ed.). (2007). *Mathematics teaching today* (2nd ed.). Reston, VA: National Council of Teachers of Mathematics.

[11] Vang, C. (2004). Teaching science to English learners. *Language Magazine, 4*(4). All of the "In my classroom" sections are adapted for each of the 5 Es with permission from *Language Magazine,* http://www.languagemagazine.com

[12] DeRuvo, S. L. (2009). *Strategies for teaching adolescents with ADHD.* San Francisco: Jossey-Bass. See p. 37.

[13] Fisher, D., & Frey, N. (2007). *Checking for understanding: Formative assessment techniques for your classroom.* Alexandria, VA: Association for Supervision and Curriculum Development.

[14] Black, P., & William, D. (1998). Inside the black box: Raising standards through classroom assessment. *Phi Delta Kappan, 80*(2), 139–149. Retrieved from http://www.pdkintl.org/kappan/kbla9810.htm

[15] Bloom, B. (1984). The 2 sigma problem: The search for methods of group instruction as effective as one-to-one tutoring. *Educational Researcher, 13*(6), 4–16. Retrieved from http://dlsystems.us/readings/NTFL_1/The_2_Sigma_Effect.pdf

[16] DeRuvo, S. L. (2009). See p. 98.

[17] Cummins, J., & Swain, M. (1986). *Bilingualism in education: Aspects of theory, research and practice.* London: Longman.

[18] Krashen, S. D. (1981). *Second language acquisition and second language learning.* New York: Pergamon; Krashen, S. D. (1985). *The input hypothesis: Issues and implications.* New York: Longman; Long, M. H. (1981). Input, interaction, and second language acquisition. *Annals of the New York Academy of Science, 379,* 259–278.

[19] Rivera, M. O., Moughamian, A. C., Lesaux, N. K., & Francis, D. J. (2009). *Language and reading interventions for English language learners and English language learners with disabilities.* Portsmouth, NH: RMC Research Corporation, Center on Instruction. Retrieved from http://www.centeroninstruction.org/files/Lang%20and%20Rdng%20Interventions%20for%20ELLs%20and%20ELLs%20with%20Disabilities.pdf

[20] Personal communication with Professor Janette Klingner, University of Colorado at Boulder.

[21] Fillmore, L. W. (1976). *The second time around: Cognitive and social strategies in second language acquisition* (Unpublished doctoral dissertation). Stanford University, Stanford, CA; Moschkovich, J. (1999). Supporting the participation of English language learners in mathematical discussions. *For the Learning of Mathematics, 19*(1), 11–19; Gibbons, P. (2002). *Scaffolding language, scaffolding learning: Teaching second language learners in the mainstream classroom.* Portsmouth, NH: Heinemann. See pp. 6–10.

[22] Anstrom, K. (1999). *Preparing secondary education teachers to work with English language learners: Mathematics* (NCBE Resource Collection Series, No. 14). Washington, DC: National Clearinghouse for Bilingual Education.

[23] Buchanan, K., & Helman, M. (1997). *Reforming mathematics instruction for ESL literacy students.* Washington, DC: ERIC Clearinghouse on Languages and Linguistics; Moschkovich, J. (1999); Cummins, J., & Swain, M. (1986).

[24] Hawkins, B. (2005). See p. 380; Bay-Williams, J. M., & Herrera, S. (2007). Is "just good teaching" enough to support the learning of English language learners? Insights from sociocultural learning theory. In W. G. Martin, M. E. Strutchens, & P. C. Elliott (Eds.), *The learning of mathematics: Sixty-ninth yearbook* (pp. 43–63). Reston, VA: National Council of Teachers of Mathematics; Freeman, D. J. (2004). Teaching in the context of English-language learners: What we need to know. In M. Sadowski (Ed.), *Teaching immigrant and second-language students: Strategies for success* (pp. 7–20). Cambridge, MA: Harvard Education Press.

[25] Slavin, R. E. (1995, October). *Research on cooperative learning and achievement: What we know, what we need to know* (No. OERI-R-117-D40005). Washington, DC: U.S. Dept. of Education. Retrieved from http://socialfamily535.pbworks.com/f/slavin1996%5B1%5D.pdf

[26] Frey, N., Fisher, D., & Everlove, S. (2009). Productive group work: How to engage students, build teamwork, and promote understanding. Alexandria, VA: Association for Supervision and Curriculum Development. See pp. 99–100.

[27] Frey, N., Fisher, D., & Everlove, S. (2009). See pp. 98–99.

[28] Winebrenner, S. (2006). *Teaching kids with learning difficulties in the regular classroom.* Minneapolis, MN: Free Spirit Publishing. See pp. 17–18, 77.

[29] McCall-Perez, Z. (2005). *Grouping English learners for science.* Unpublished manuscript. Adapted with permission.

[30] Cohen, E. G. (1994). *Designing groupwork: Strategies for the heterogeneous classroom.* New York: Teachers College Press.

CHAPTER 2

Getting to Know Students with Learning Difficulties

> Diversity is a gold mine. It offers all members of a diverse group multiple ideas, perspectives, and solutions to problems. Teachers can nurture this diversity early on by maximizing the potential of each student in their classrooms, including students who come to the class with defined disabilities. And practicing differentiated instruction, matching teaching to the needs of each learner, is an ideal way to help diversity thrive.

— Jennifer Carolan and Abigail Guinn

This chapter describes characteristics of the more prevalent types of students with learning difficulties — students who can benefit tremendously from the kind of teaching organized by the 5 Es framework introduced in chapter 1. The information we provide on students with certain learning difficulties — usually called learning *disabilities* in special education — is meant to help general education teachers better understand these students who want very much to learn but struggle mightily in core academic subjects.

Chapter 3 presents information about English learners, another group of students who can benefit from the teaching approaches advocated in this guidebook, and that chapter is meant to help special education teachers better understand the language development of their students who are English learners with learning difficulties, particularly those with language processing difficulties.

The number of students with special needs receiving education within general education classrooms has increased because of federal legislation — particularly the most recent versions of the Elementary and Secondary Education Act (ESEA) and the Individuals with Disabilities Education Act (IDEA).[1] State and local educational agencies are responsible for meeting the educational needs of an increasingly diverse student population, and ESEA programs must provide a wide range of resources and support to ensure that all students have the opportunity to succeed in college and in a career. As more students with learning difficulties are served in inclusive settings — the least restrictive environment — teachers need research-based strategies that help students to be academically and socially successful.

Students with learning difficulties have the right to access core instruction in the least restrictive environment. Federal law requires that districts ensure access to the general education curriculum to the maximum extent possible.[2] In IDEA, the general education curriculum is defined as "the same curriculum as for nondisabled children." It is the goal of special education to meet the challenge of providing access to the general education curriculum through an array of learning opportunities that lead to academic success and postsecondary options that are available to all students. Students who are designated for special education have the ability to learn, and their ability may even be higher than that of their peers who do not have learning difficulties if they are taught in the ways they learn best. With proper planning and implementation, differentiated instruction in a general education classroom can benefit both students with learning difficulties and their peers who do not have identified learning difficulties.

To effectively teach students with learning difficulties, general education teachers need to know about the characteristics — the strengths and challenges — of students with learning difficulties. It is important to keep in mind that each student with a learning difficulty is a unique person, as are students without learning difficulties. All students have strengths and challenges, learning preferences, and personal interests. Knowing about how students with (and without) learning difficulties learn is the starting point for thinking about ways to tailor the classroom environment and instructional strategies to fit all students' learning needs.

This chapter provides an overview of the typical characteristics of students with learning difficulties that frequently interfere with success in academics. Rather than attempting to address all types of learning difficulties, this guidebook focuses on particular types that comprise a high percentage of the students who receive at least some of their special education services within a general education setting. In other words, this guidebook focuses on students with learning difficulties who receive instruction on grade-level academic standards the same as their general education peers. Also, we assume that many students who have these particular learning difficulties are undiagnosed or are diagnosed but do not qualify to receive special education services, so they are placed in general education classrooms.

As stated earlier, what we call learning *difficulties* is usually called *disabilities* in IDEA special education codes; for us, *difficulties* connotes the expectation that all students can achieve at high levels when we find the teaching strategies and muster the resources that they need to be successful. We are not alone in preferring the term *difficulties*,[3] as it best adheres to the accepted principle that all students can learn.

Figure 2.1 lists the main types of learning difficulties that we focus on in this book and the acronyms we use for them.

FIGURE 2.1. **Reference Guide to Acronyms for Learning Difficulties**	
SLD	Specific Learning Difficulty
ADHD	Attention Deficit Hyperactivity Disorder
AS	Asperger Syndrome (part of autism spectrum disorder)

STUDENTS WITH SPECIFIC LEARNING DIFFICULTIES

According to IDEA (2004), a specific learning disability (which we refer to as a specific learning *difficulty*) is:

> A disorder in one or more of the basic psychological processes involved in understanding or in using language, spoken or written, that may manifest itself in an imperfect ability to listen, think, speak, read, write, spell, or to do mathematical calculations, including conditions such as perceptual disabilities, brain injury, minimal brain dysfunction, dyslexia, and developmental aphasia.[4]

SLD is a term that describes specific kinds of processing problems that affect a broad range of academic skills. Because the specific difficulties experienced by individual students will vary, the term may be referred to as covering a mixed bag of difficulties. An SLD manifests itself as a difficulty in one or more of the following areas: attention, reasoning, processing, memory, communication, reading, writing, spelling, calculation, coordination, social competence, and emotional maturity. According to the U.S. Department of Education's National Center for Education Statistics (NCES, 2010), slightly more than 40 percent of students with disabilities are being served under this category.

Nationwide, 40 percent of all students in special education have reading as their core challenge. It is the academic area in which most students with an SLD are challenged — nationwide, more than 80 percent of students with an SLD struggle with reading.[5] The reading difficulty often may be traced to dyslexia, difficulty understanding both oral and written words and sentences. Students with dyslexia have problems decoding and translating printed words into spoken words and have difficulty with reading comprehension. It is the most common cause of reading, writing, and spelling difficulties. Problems in reading typically interfere with student performance in all academic areas, especially at the secondary level where procedural recall demands are replaced primarily with declarative skills that require more complex comprehension of information, solving word problems, and conceptual understanding.[6] Approximately four of every five students with SLDs perform significantly below grade level in reading.[7] Students with SLDs struggle to decode text because of difficulties with letter recognition and letter-sound correspondence. In addition, students with SLDs often lack sufficient vocabulary to quickly connect what they are reading to background knowledge and personal experiences. For example, a student needs to be able to read and understand content-specific vocabulary such as *rationalize* and *square root* to be literate in mathematics. Reading difficulties may also contribute to difficulties in written expression because reading skills tend to develop before comparable writing skills. For example, writing difficulties can interfere with writing a summary of a history text in a paragraph format. Typically, students who are significantly below grade level in reading will also be below grade level in written expression. However, some students with SLDs who have problems with *written* expression are proficient *readers* nonetheless.

Many students with SLDs who have specific difficulties in mathematics may or may not have specific difficulties in reading. As with students' reading difficulties, math difficulties range from mild to severe. It is estimated that 6 to 7 percent of school-age students exhibit difficulties in some area of mathematics. For instance, some students have an excellent grasp of math concepts but are inconsistent in calculating. They inconsistently pay attention to the operational sign, have trouble borrowing or carrying appropriately, or inconsistently sequence the steps in complex operations. Often these students may experience difficulty mastering basic number facts or remembering a sequence of steps. There are two major areas of weakness that can contribute to such challenges:

» Visual-spatial difficulties, which result in a student having trouble processing what the eyes see; and

» Language processing difficulties, which result in a student having trouble processing and making sense of what the ears hear.

"Poor memory" is one of the most frequently noted problems among students with SLDs. For example, a difficulty establishing easily accessible long-term memories may manifest itself when a student attempts to rapidly retrieve information learned, such as basic number facts, conventions for naming different chemical compounds, or basic grammatical rules. Another area of difficulty may be working memory. Working memory, sometimes called short-term memory, is the ability to actively hold information in the mind needed to do complex tasks such as reasoning, comprehending, making inferences, and following a complex sequence of procedures. It is the ability to notice something, think about it, and then act on this information as required.

Students with SLDs may have visual processing problems such as difficulties with visual-spatial skills.[8] For example, a student with a visual-spatial difficulty may lose his or her place on a worksheet, experience difficulty differentiating between numbers or symbols, have difficulty writing in a straight line or in columns, struggle with the directional aspects in math, such as in problems involving left-right (regrouping) or aligning of numbers, or completing a classification chart for science.

In addition, many students with SLDs have central auditory processing difficulties. *Auditory processing* is a term used to describe what happens when your brain recognizes and interprets the sounds around you. Having an auditory processing difficulty means that something is adversely affecting the processing or interpretation of the information coming in. Students with auditory processing difficulties may struggle to participate in oral drills or comprehend a teacher's explanation of complex procedures. In other words, students with auditory processing disorders can hear normally but their minds cannot sort or make sense of everything they hear.[9] Auditory processing disorders are also prevalent in other learning disabilities, such as students with ADHD or AS.

Response to Intervention

Response to Intervention (RTI) is a relatively new process or framework for evaluating students for special education under the SLD category.

RTI has emerged as an alternative to what is often called the "discrepancy model" for identifying students for special education under the SLD category. Prior to the reauthorization of IDEA in 2004, schools traditionally diagnosed students with a specific learning disability (Education Code term) when there was a significant discrepancy between a test of their intelligence quotient (IQ) and their performance on individually administered tests of a broad range of academic skills. Since the reauthorization of IDEA in 2004 (specifically, Section 300.307 of the Special Education Regulations), states have been given the option to adopt criteria other than the traditional discrepancy model.

RTI allows for school personnel to assess special education eligibility for a specific learning disability based on lack of "response to intervention" rather than by diagnostically assessing the presence of a learning disability.[10] The intent of RTI is to address the needs of children who are struggling within the core content areas (specifically in the areas of mathematics, reading, and writing) by identifying students who are not making expected progress, implementing research-based interventions proven to ameliorate the high hurdles to learning, and monitoring students' progress to determine if the interventions are working for particular students.

Often RTI has three tiers for providing comprehensive support to students. Below is an example of a three-level RTI system, but the number of tiers and the RTI process can vary. Students are placed into tiers based on results of comprehensive assessments such as universal screening and progress monitoring tools.

» In Tier 1, the general education teacher implements high-quality, research-based strategies for the whole class, including differentiated instruction in the core curriculum, and monitors students' progress. Any students who do not progress at the same rate as the majority (e.g., 80 percent or more) of the class may need further intervention.

» In Tier 2, the general education teacher or a specialist (e.g., special education, reading specialist, EL specialist) provides evidenced-based, moderately intensive interventions that address the learning or behavioral challenges of the students identified in Tier 1 as needing more intensive support.[11] There is no formula for how long Tier 2 interventions should last, but progress should be monitored frequently, at least every four to six weeks, to evaluate how well the interventions are working.[12]

» In Tier 3, a student who shows minimal or no progress with the first two levels of intervention receives individualized, intensive instruction that focuses on the student's strengths while targeting the student's needs, or "skill deficits." A student who still does not make progress over an extended period of time may be referred for comprehensive evaluation and considered for special education services under IDEA 2004.

At all levels, attention is placed on fidelity of implementation, with consideration of students' strengths and of cultural and linguistic responsiveness. The duration, intensity, and frequency of these tiered interventions vary according to the needs of the students and the fidelity of the programs being used. The teaching framework described in chapter 1 and the language and scaffolding strategies described in chapters 4 and 5 could be a school's Tier 1 core instructional strategies for all diverse learners in an inclusive classroom.

STUDENTS WITH ATTENTION DEFICIT HYPERACTIVITY DISORDER

ADHD is an often misunderstood condition characterized by problems of inattention, hyperactivity, and/or impulsivity. According to the American Psychiatric Association's *Diagnostic and Statistical Manual of Mental Disorders*, "The essential feature of ADHD is a persistent pattern of inattention and/or hyperactivity-impulsivity that is more frequent and severe than is typically observed in individuals at a comparable level of development."[13] According to experts, ADHD affects 3 to 7 percent of the population.[14]

The current diagnosis for ADHD is divided into four categories.[15] The categorical diagnosis depends on the student's most predominant behavior. The four categories and the manifested behaviors are:

1. ADHD, Combined Type: A student who exhibits inattention and hyperactivity, but not significant impulsivity. The student often has difficulty sustaining attention and becomes easily distracted.

2. ADHD, Predominantly Inattentive Type: A student who exhibits inattention, but neither hyperactivity nor impulsivity. The student may be viewed as a daydreamer or an underachiever. These students typically are under the radar of the teacher due to exhibiting passive characteristics.

3. ADHD, Predominantly Hyperactive-Impulsive Type: A student who exhibits both hyperactivity and impulsivity that is maladaptive and inconsistent with his or her developmental level and usually exhibits no inattention. The student may be constantly in motion, talking excessively, having difficulty awaiting a turn, and/or having difficulty interpreting others.[16] These students typically are of concern to teachers because of their potential to disrupt others in class and because they require continual and consistent monitoring from the teacher.

4. ADHD, Not Otherwise Specified: A student who doesn't meet the full criteria for ADHD but exhibits some of the symptoms.

While an SLD affects just one or two cognitive functions, ADHD tends to affect learning globally and compromise all cognitive functions. Generally speaking, parents will report difficulties at home of a similar nature to difficulties at school reported by a student's teachers. Although other learning difficulties are often diagnosed by the school system, ADHD cannot be. ADHD is a medical, neurological condition, so only medical professionals can make the diagnosis. Students with ADHD may qualify for special education services if the disorder affects learning in all academic areas. Many students diagnosed with ADHD qualify for special education services under IDEA and are classified under the category of "other health impairment" because behavior problems affect their academic progress.[17] And some students with ADHD do not qualify for special education programs at all. Numerous federal laws support the least restrictive environment (general education placement) for students with ADHD.[18]

For most students diagnosed with ADHD, the foremost characteristic is the inability to regulate attention, rather than inattention. The inability to self-regulate attention can be subdivided into five types:

1. Divided attention — the inability to complete two tasks simultaneously (for example, difficulty taking notes while paying attention to a visual presentation).

2. Focused attention — the inability to attend to the task at hand (for example, preoccupied with organizing a notebook instead of what is being discussed).

3. Selective attention — the inability to ignore competing or irrelevant stimuli (for example, distracted by the noise of a student entering or exiting the room).

4. Sustained attention — the inability to maintain attention to a task long enough to sufficiently complete the task (for example, moving on to the next task before completing the first assigned task).

5. Vigilance and readiness to respond — the inability to have vigilance and readiness to respond (for example, reacting before completion of instructions for an activity).

Executive functioning — skills that enable us to carry out the mental activities that help regulate our behavior — is critical to maintaining attention for the time it takes to attain a future goal or react appropriately to a novel situation.[19] The inability to regulate attention is a symptom of weak executive functioning. ADHD is fundamentally a deficit in executive functioning.[20] There are two ways that executive functioning helps everyone to regulate behavior — thinking and behavior skills. First, a person with strong executive functioning can focus attention long enough to apply certain thinking skills to accomplish a task. Second, a person with strong executive functioning can regulate behavior to achieve the targeted goal; in other words, the person thinks before acting. We depend on executive functioning to perform daily activities such as planning, organizing, strategizing, paying attention to and remembering details, and managing time and space. Figure 2.2 presents characteristics of executive functioning specific to thinking and behavior skills.[21]

FIGURE 2.2. Thinking and Behavior Skills Associated with Executive Functioning

Executive Functioning	
Thinking Skills	**Behavior Skills**
Planning – being able to think about a goal and plan for how to attain it	Response inhibition – being able to stop one's own behavior, including actions and thoughts, at the appropriate time
Organization – being able to design and maintain systems for keeping track of information or materials	Emotional control – being able to self-regulate emotional responses
Time management – being able to recognize time available, how to allocate it, and how to stay within time limits and deadlines	Sustained attention – being able to attend to a situation or task when distracted, bored, or fatigued
Working memory – being able to actively hold information in the mind for the time needed to do complex tasks; the ability to see something, think about it, and then act on this information as required	Task initiation – being able to begin a task in a timely fashion
	Flexibility – being able to change or adjust to conditions when necessary
Metacognition – being aware of your own learning, how you learn best, and how successful you are at completing a task (e.g., How am I doing? How did I do?)	Goal-directed persistence – being able follow through to complete a goal

Because ADHD is linked to general weaknesses in executive functioning, it can affect a student's ability to learn in all academic areas. The greatest academic difficulty for students with ADHD is the ability to produce written work.[22] Some form of writing is required for almost all academic courses. Students with ADHD may have mastered the content knowledge but struggle with the ability to organize their thoughts and attend to the cognitive task long enough to produce a written product. Writing difficulties also impact the areas of spelling and grammar because these skills require attention to detail.[23] Many students with ADHD have difficulty reading lengthy text passages with comprehension, and some may have difficulty with charts, graphs, and symbols. For these students, the difficulty is not decoding the text — it is maintaining executive functioning long enough to be able to construct new ideas presented in the text, organize the new ideas, and relate them to existing knowledge. It is important to recognize that particular areas of weaknesses in executive functioning skills are also characteristic of students with Asperger syndrome/autism spectrum disorder.

Academic courses may also be difficult for students with ADHD when the teacher requires students to multitask, for example, asking students to take notes while listening and watching a video.

STUDENTS WITH ASPERGER SYNDROME

Asperger syndrome (AS) is characterized as a neurological disorder that affects children with average to high intelligence, affecting particularly their ability to socialize and communicate effectively with others. It is classified as one of five pervasive developmental disorders.[24] Asperger syndrome is grouped under the broader category called autism spectrum disorder, or ASD. It is estimated that 1 in every 100 children in the United States is diagnosed with ASD, and the incidence is growing.[25] In order to keep terms as simple as possible and focus on what general education teachers most need to know, we use the acronym AS to refer to *both* Asperger syndrome and high-functioning ASD even though we recognize that there is no formal diagnosis called "high-functioning ASD."[26]

Students with AS typically have high intelligence and exhibit differences in severity in terms of communication, socialization, patterns of behavior and interests, sensory processing, emotional regulation, and thinking and learning.[27] Other cognitive areas may be affected as well, including sensory-motor processing, learning, thinking abstractly, making and understanding inferences, and recognizing when something is not to be taken literally (e.g., "it's raining cats and dogs"). There are three common specific characteristics: difficulty with communication, problems with socialization, and restricted patterns of behavior.[28] However, no two persons with AS have the same profile of symptoms, onset, or prognosis. A common characteristic of people with AS is their weak social skills and needing to be explicitly taught how to interact with peers. For example, a person with AS may not pick up on the meaning of another person's facial expression or intonation or be able to judge how much to say or what to say as appropriate responses. This is important for teachers to know when forming small groups to perform tasks that require negotiating ideas.

Children with AS usually appear to be developing normally in terms of expressive speech, motor development, and basic self-help skills. But between the ages of 4 and 8 years, there will usually be an apparent difficulty in the use of nonverbal language, such as little, no, or unusual eye contact with the other person in a conversation and an absence of or rare interest in what others are doing or saying around them. It is more prevalent among boys than girls (ratio of four males to one female), but an increasing number of girls are being identified as having AS.

Central auditory processing disorders are commonly observed in students with AS, as well as for students with SLD and ADHD. Students with AS that have central auditory processing disorders can exhibit extreme responses to sounds and noises. They may respond with pain, anxiety, and panic because they have hyperacute hearing. Hearing affects not only how they perceive and understand the sounds they hear but also their abilities to focus and attend, regulate sensory stimulation, develop appropriate speech and language skills, develop socially, and organize, plan, and sequence.[29]

Students with AS exhibit weaknesses in executive functioning.[30] Students with AS may have more severe executive functioning weaknesses in task initiation, working memory, metacognition, and flexibility compared with students with ADHD or SLD. In particular, students with AS tend to have difficulty dealing with transitions and unexpected changes in their schedules and routines. They may compensate by exhibiting "learned helplessness," needing prompts to remind them to get out materials and supplies to begin work or waiting for direct instructions to begin or complete a task. A common pitfall occurs when teachers perform the executive functioning tasks for students rather than helping them learn to perform the tasks for themselves. However, a classroom environment that is predictable and has established routines, procedures, and protocols can provide the structure to support students with weaknesses in executive functioning skills to become self-reliant individuals.

AS is often accompanied by these characteristics:[31]

> » Selective listening (e.g., attending to the sound of a clock ticking instead of a peer interactive conversation)

> » Difficulty learning expressive language (e.g., improper use of tenses)

> » Echolalia (e.g., repeating back what you have heard word-by-word)

> » Perseverating behavior and rituals (e.g., difficulty adjusting to changes in routine or familiar surroundings)

> » Self-stimulatory behavior (e.g., hand-flapping, rocking, spinning)

> » Specific and unusual fears (e.g., afraid of the sound of a flushing toilet)

COMPARISON OF STUDENTS WITH SLD, ADHD, AND AS

Figure 2.3 presents some common academic characteristics of students with learning difficulties.[32] This chart is meant as a guide to help general education teachers recognize and understand students with special needs and collaborate with special education teachers on instructional strategies that fit the students' characteristics. These strengths and challenges may reflect many, but certainly not all, students with the learning difficulty; and the chart should not be used in place of formal diagnostic instruments. Many other characteristics specific to reading, writing, speaking, or listening could be listed, but we have kept the chart relatively simple in order for it to be most useful as a quick reference.

By "common" characteristics, we mean characteristics that are often present for the majority of students within a type of learning difficulty, but not always present or to the same extent. Some characteristics are common or similar across two or three types of learning difficulties, whereas other characteristics are fairly unique to a single type of learning difficulty. Some characteristics are considered strengths of the student; others

FIGURE 2.3. Characteristics of Students with Learning Difficulties Across Domains*

Students with SLD	Students with ADHD	Students with AS
Strengths	**Strengths**	**Strengths**
Learning visually	Learning visually	Learning visually
Thinking concretely, literally, logically	Thinking creatively, critically	Thinking flexibly, critically
Comprehending main ideas	Having strong factual knowledge	Retaining and recalling factual knowledge (e.g., details, facts)
Following agreed-upon rules/roles for discussions	Sustaining attention in high-interest topics of conversation	Sustaining attention
	Discussing ideas	Initiating social interactions with adults and peers (but may do so awkwardly)
	Initiating social interactions with peers	Acquiring and using vocabulary (not multiple meanings)
	Drawing, painting	Having precocious, fluent reading skills (e.g., decoding)
		Following agreed-upon rules/roles for discussions
Challenges	**Challenges**	**Challenges**
Summarizing/organizing information	Summarizing/organizing information	Summarizing/organizing information
Organizing ideas	Organizing	Organizing
Generalizing strategies to other situations	Generalizing strategies to other situations	Initiating task without prompts
Remembering what is heard orally	Sustaining attention to complete a task	Generalizing strategies to other situations
Reasoning	Following time limits, waiting, using unstructured time	Making inferences, judgments; understanding others' points of view
Acquiring and using vocabulary	Following multistep tasks	Avoiding thinking literally/rigidly
Following multistep tasks	Following agreed-upon rules/roles for discussions	Following time limits
Following writing conventions	Following writing conventions	Following multistep tasks
Avoiding visual-spatial difficulties	Handwriting; aligning numbers	Communicating ideas
	Self-regulating thoughts or emotions	Following writing conventions
		Handwriting; aligning numbers
		Having hyper-/hyposensitivity to stimuli (sounds, odors, tactile)

* Common characteristics found in research that may or may not apply to each individual.

are challenges for the student to overcome over time. The teacher of a student with a learning difficulty should teach to the student's strengths and avoid the student's challenges or work with the student on those challenges as appropriate. For example, the teacher might use graphic organizers to work on the student's challenge of "seeing" relationships between main ideas or a main idea and all of its supporting evidence or details. The student with AS can be quite a rigid thinker and is comforted by class routines, so the teacher should alert the student ahead of time of a change in routine and usually the student will feel prepared and go along with it.

Teachers should bear in mind that there are so much besides just these academic characteristics that make up the whole child as an individual. Teachers also should remember that students with learning difficulties want to learn and can learn with appropriate support. Disruptive or passive behavior may be a student's way of sending a message that things are going terribly wrong for the student.

The chart (Figure 2.3) can be used as a checklist and to create a profile of a student. When a particular student exhibits some characteristics of different types of learning difficulties, it may be that the student has a combination of learning difficulties. Ideally a special education teacher would create the student profile and, with the student's general education teachers, discuss the instructional strategies that best fit the student's needs.

INDIVIDUALIZED EDUCATION PROGRAM FOR A STUDENT WITH DUAL DESIGNATION

This section is for special education teachers who have dually designated students—students who are English learners *and* have learning difficulties. These students need research-based instruction in English language development *and* course content that addresses their learning difficulties. These dually designated students should have English Language Proficiency (ELP) standards embedded in their individualized education programs (IEPs). Chapter 3 presents charts of ELP standards for the general and special education teacher to see the expected student performance across five proficiency levels across grade spans; but teachers should use the standards adopted by their state (the state may use the term *ELP* or *ELD*).

We recommend that special education teachers collaborate with English language development specialists (e.g., ELD/ESL teachers) and speech/language specialists (who have cross-cultural, cross-language competency) to select ELP standards (a state might use the term *indicators* as specific descriptors of generally stated standards) at the proficiency level just above the student's current performance. The standards can be short-term objectives or perhaps long-term goals; an ELD/ESL specialist can help identify how long it will likely take for the student to become proficient at that next level. We recommend that an IEP include a cohesive set of content standards that involve critical thinking, arguably the most important of the standards that address understanding and communicating main ideas. Then the IEP should embed the ELP standards regarding the communication of main ideas that an English learner needs to develop.

Many students with learning difficulties have difficulty with social skills as well as appropriately communicating their ideas. Having dual designation as an English learner exacerbates the challenges. IEPs for these students should include social skills, goals and explicit instruction, especially targeting skills needed to participate in a small group on an academic task during a lesson. This is a basis for the special education teacher to alert the general education teacher about a student's needs and collaborate on ways to teach the student how to interact in a small group to accomplish academic tasks.

ENDNOTES FOR CHAPTER 2

[1] Heller, R., & Greenleaf, C. (2007). *Literacy instruction in the content areas: Getting to the core of middle and high school improvement.* Washington, DC: Alliance for Excellent Education.

[2] IDEA (34CFR §300.320(a)(1)(i)).

[3] For example, see: Winebrenner, S. (2006). *Teaching kids with learning difficulties in the regular classroom.* Minneapolis, MN: Free Spirit Publishing.

[4] Individuals with Disabilities Education Act, 20 U.S.C. 104, section 602 (30) (A) (2004).

[5] Levenson, N. (2011). *Something has got to change: Rethinking special education.* Washington, DC: American Enterprise Institute for Public Policy Research. Retrieved from http://www.aei.org/papers/education/something-has-got-to-change-rethinking-special-education

[6] Steele, M. (2010, Summer). High school students with learning disabilities: Mathematics instruction, study skills, and high stakes tests. *American Secondary Education, 38*(3), 21–27.

[7] Rosenberg, M. S., Westling, D. L., & McLeskey, J. (2008). *Special education for today's teachers: An introduction.* Columbus, OH: Merrill.

[8] Bender, W. (2008a). *Learning disabilities: Characteristics, identification, and teaching strategies.* Columbus, OH: Merrill.

[9] Bashe, P. R., & Kirby, B. L. (2005). *The OASIS guide to Asperger syndrome: Advice, support, insight, and inspiration.* New York: Crowne Publishing. See pp. 192–194.

[10] Hawken, L. S., Vincent, C. G., & Schumann, J. (2008). Response to intervention for social behavior: Challenges and opportunities. *Journal of Emotional and Behavioral Disorders, 16*(4), 213–225. See p. 213.

[11] National Center on Response to Intervention. (n.d.). *The essential components of RTI.* Retrieved from http://www.rti4success.org/whatisrti

[12] RTI Action Network. (n.d.). *What is RTI?* Retrieved from http://www.rtinetwork.org/learn/what/whatisrti

[13] American Psychiatric Association. (2000). *Diagnostic and statistical manual of mental disorders* (4th ed., text rev.). Washington, DC: Author. See p. 85.

[14] Vaughn, B., & Kratochvil, C. (2006). Pharmacotherapy of ADHD in young children. *Psychiatry, 3*(8), 36–45.

[15] Lougy, R., DeRuvo, S., & Rosenthal, D. (2007). *Teaching young children with ADHD: Successful strategies and practical interventions for preK–3.* Thousand Oaks, CA: Corwin Press. See pp. 2–3.

[16] Friend, M., & Bursuck, W. (2002). *Including students with special needs: A practical guide for classroom teachers.* Needham Heights, MA: Allyn & Bacon. See pp. 236–242.

[17] Students who have ADHD but do not qualify for special education services may be entitled to accommodations and modifications in the category "other health impaired" under Section 504 of the Rehabilitation Act of 1973.

[18] Nowacek, E. J., & Mamlin, N. (2007, Spring). General education teachers and students with ADHD: What modifications are made? *Preventing School Failure, 51*(3), 28.

[19] Schetter, P. (2004). *Learning the R.O.P.E.S. for improved executive function: A cognitive behavioral approach for individuals with high functioning autism and other behavioral disorders.* Redding, CA: ABTA. See p. 1.

[20] Barkley, R. A. (1997). *ADHD and the nature of self-control.* New York: Guilford Press.

[21] Dawson, P., & Guare, R. (2010). *Executive skills in children and adolescents: A practical guide to assessment and intervention.* New York: Guilford Press.

[22] Lougy, R., DeRuvo, S., & Rosenthal, D. (2007).

[23] Pittman, G. (2011, August 23). Writing problems common in kids with ADHD. ABS-CBNNews.com. Retrieved from http://www.abs-cbnnews.com/lifestyle/08/23/11/writing-problems-common-kids-adhd

[24] Listed in *Diagnostic and statistical manual of mental disorders* (American Psychiatric Association, 2000) as a pervasive developmental disorder.

[25] Cassidy, S., Ramirez, D., Bakken, C., Gadzuk, N., & Alvarez-Martini, M. (2011). Students enrolled in California public schools diagnosed with autism. *The Multilingual Educator*, 34–38. Retrieved from http://wexford.org/wexford_files_files/CABE%20Autism%20Article.pdf

[26] Ozonoff, S., & Griffith, E. M. (2000). Neuropsychological function and the external validity of Asperger syndrome. In A. Klin, F. R. Volkmar, & S. S. Sparrow (Eds.), *Asperger syndrome* (pp. 72–96). New York: Guildford Press.

[27] National Professional Development Center on Autism Spectrum Disorders. (2008a). Session 1: Understanding pervasive developmental disorders and autism spectrum disorder. In *Foundations of autism spectrum disorders: An online course.* Chapel Hill, NC: FPG Child Development Institute, University of North Carolina.

[28] Schetter, P. (2004).

[29] Bashe, P. R., & Kirby, B. L. (2005). See p. 193.

[30] Ozonoff, S., & Griffith, E. M. (2000).

[31] National Professional Development Center on Autism Spectrum Disorders. (2008b). Session 2: Characteristics of learners with autism spectrum disorders. In *Foundations of autism spectrum disorders: An online course.* Chapel Hill: FPG Child Development Institute, University of North Carolina.

[32] Bashe, P. R., & Kirby, B. L. (2005). See pp. 9–82; Bergeson, T., Davidson, C., Harmon, B., Gill, D. H., & Colwell, M. L. (2008). *The educational aspects of autism spectrum disorders.* Olympia, WA: Special Education, Office of Superintendent of Public Instruction. Retrieved from www.k12.wa.us/SpecialEd/pubdocs/Autism%20Manual.pdf. See pp. 1–71; National Professional Development Center on Autism Spectrum Disorders. (2008a, 2008b); Cassidy, S., Ramirez, D., Bakken, C., Gadzuk, N., & Alvarez-Martini, M. (2011). See pp. 34–38; Schetter, P. (2004); Lougy, R., DeRuvo, S., & Rosenthal, D. (2007).

Getting to Know English Learners

> "Language is the air that we breathe and the water in which we swim. It comes as naturally to us as seeing the sky or digesting our food. But what if we suddenly had to breathe different air or swim in different waters? ... If we had to think about not only what we say but also how to say it, the language overload would be exhausting."
>
> — Jane Hill and Kathleen Flynn

Students who are English learners face unique challenges in school, often struggling with "language overload" as so much of their education transpires through the medium of a language in which they are not yet fluent. But every English learner is unique and — just like any other student — has the potential to enrich the classroom with personal strengths, interests, and experiences. Given the right support, they can learn at the highest academic levels.

English learners differ from one another on many factors, such as formal schooling in their country of origin, similarities between their primary language and English (e.g., written language, grammar), parent and student aspirations, culture, and learning styles and difficulties. This chapter focuses mainly on how English learners can be characterized in terms of the stages, or levels, of their second language acquisition, with a focus on academic language. People do not learn language all at once. Instead, their use and comprehension of vocabulary and grammatical structures gradually increase over time.

English learners face language challenges that overlap with the challenges that some other students face in reading and writing. English learners struggle to decode or comprehend English written texts until they reach a certain level of proficiency — having acquired sufficient vocabulary and decoding and comprehension skills to read fluently and with understanding. But it would be a disservice to simply place English learners in an intervention program for struggling readers and ignore how they are different from native English speakers who also struggle with reading.

Researchers Short and Fitzsimmons aptly contrasted important differences between adolescent struggling readers who are native English-speaking versus those who are struggling readers and English learners.[1]

» Whereas native English-speaking students may have been unsuccessful learning to read or reading to learn, some English learners make progress influenced by their speed of acquiring English and some were never taught to read in their country of origin.

» Whereas native English-speaking students have a relatively wide vocabulary range and multiple meanings of certain words, English learners need much more vocabulary development, including multiple meanings of words and high-priority academic words that are cross-disciplinary.

» Students born in the United States are likely to understand many U.S. cultural and historical references, while English learners who entered the United States recently must build more background knowledge in order to understand these kinds of references.

In this guidebook we focus on strategies that are effective for all diverse learners, but we adhere to the notion that every student is unique, and therefore it is important for district and school leaders as well as general and special education teachers and specialists to understand the particular characteristics of English learners in order to best support these students.

Knowing at least some information about an English learner's native language is one way a teacher can better understand the student and how to help the student learn. Teachers can benefit from being aware of at least some similarities and dissimilarities between English and a student's primary language, such as the writing system and grammar. The greater the difference between the primary language and English, the more likely the student will struggle until the student is proficient enough to "think in English" without needing to work back and forth through the primary language. This may be oversimplifying linguistics and second language development theory, but the intent is to say that different primary languages can have differential influence on the speed and ease with which a student learns English. The more proficient a student is in his or her primary language, the better equipped the student is to learn the sounds, letters, rules, and such of the second language. A person literate in English can learn to "read" Spanish in minutes, but of course cannot comprehend it without knowledge of Spanish vocabulary, idioms, and so on. These two ideas can be summarized as follows: The more a student knows about his or her primary language and the more similar a primary language's words and grammatical structures are to English, the faster and easier it is to learn English as a second language.

ENGLISH LANGUAGE PROFICIENCY LEVELS

In order to best support content learning within each student's zone of proximal development, teachers will want to know the academic history of their English learners and have a clear understanding of each student's English language proficiency (ELP) level.[2] The five levels used in this guidebook—*Entering, Emerging, Developing, Expanding,* and *Bridging* — represent distinctions often made in ELP standards.

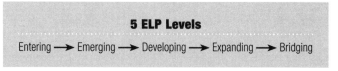

5 ELP Levels

Entering → Emerging → Developing → Expanding → Bridging

Some states use terminology that is different from what we use in this guidebook — for instance, using the term *English language development* (ELD) instead of ELP.[3] But the general idea of progressing from novice to expert in English remains the same.

In this chapter, we describe the characteristics of each ELP level by providing charts with performance indicators, which are descriptors of what a typical student at a given ELP level can say or do. Some states may use the term *benchmarks* or the term *standards* instead of *performance indicators*. We follow the terminology of ELP standards and performance indicators promoted by World-Class Instructional Design and Assessment (WIDA) and by Teachers of English to Speakers of Other Languages (TESOL) and adopted or adapted by many states.[4] We consider these to be the foremost language or literacy skills for English learners to access the content of core disciplines (English language arts, science, mathematics, and social science). Teachers should check their state ELP standards to see all language and literacy skills English learners are expected to learn as they progress toward proficiency on English language arts standards.

Figure 3.1 on page 42 shows the typical language characteristics of English learners at each of the five ELP levels. The chart generalizes across grades 1–12 and across the domains of listening, speaking, reading, and writing. The language characteristics in the left column are from TESOL resources. The chart offers general teaching strategies in the right column, which are more fully described in other chapters.

FIGURE 3.1. K–12 Language Characteristics and Teaching Strategies

Language Characteristics	Teaching Strategies
L1: Entering Students initially have limited or no understanding of English. They rarely use English for communication. They respond nonverbally to simple commands, statements, and questions. As their oral comprehension increases, they begin to imitate the verbalizations of others by using single words or simple phrases, and they begin to use English spontaneously. At the earliest stage, these learners construct meaning from text primarily through illustrations, graphs, maps, and tables.	Use target vocabulary and sentence structure based on students' comprehension; repeat and rephrase; accompany oral instruction with visuals and hands-on activities. Make connections to students' prior personal and academic experiences. Ask basic, factual questions that can be answered with gestures or a few words. Address various learning modalities. Categorize learned words on wall charts, by concept, for easy reference. Use brief texts with pictures at students' readability level. Provide mostly completed chapter outlines (include small pictures of key words when possible) with a few blanks for students to complete. Scaffold writing (such as with models, Sentence Frames). Assess students orally and perhaps use Sentence Frames, labeled graphic organizers, and illustrations.
L2: Emerging Students can understand phrases and short sentences. They can communicate limited information in simple everyday and routine situations by using memorized phrases, groups of words, and formulae. They can use selected simple structures correctly but still systematically produce basic errors. Students begin to use general academic vocabulary and familiar everyday expressions. Errors in writing are present that often hinder communication.	Use vocabulary and sentence structure based on students' comprehension; repeat and rephrase; accompany oral instruction with visuals and hands-on activities. Make connections to students' prior personal and academic experiences. Ask fairly basic, factual questions that can be answered with a few words or simple phrases. Address various learning modalities. Categorize learned words on wall charts, by concept, for easy reference. Use texts with pictures at students' readability level. Provide partially completed chapter outlines with about 8–12 blanks for students to complete. Scaffold writing (such as with models, Sentence Frames). Assess students using graphic organizers and moderately supportive Sentence Frames.
L3: Developing Students understand more complex speech but still may require some repetition. They use English spontaneously but may have difficulty expressing all their thoughts due to a restricted vocabulary and a limited command of language structure. Students at this level speak in simple sentences, which are comprehensible and appropriate, but which are frequently marked by grammatical errors. Proficiency in reading may vary considerably. Students are most successful constructing meaning from texts for which they have background knowledge upon which to build.	Choose vocabulary and sentence structure based on students' comprehension; repeat and rephrase as needed; accompany oral instruction with visuals and hands-on activities. Make connections to students' prior personal and academic experiences. Ask critical thinking questions that can be answered with phrases and simple sentences. Address various learning modalities. Provide texts at students' readability level. Teach students to use glossaries and their vocabulary notes as references. Provide models and less scaffolding for writing. Assess students using Sentence Frames/Starters; follow with specific oral prompting for ambiguities.

Language Characteristics	Teaching Strategies
L4: Expanding Students' language skills are adequate for most day-to-day communication needs. They communicate in English in new or unfamiliar settings but have occasional difficulty with complex structures and abstract academic concepts. Students at this level may read with considerable fluency and are able to locate and identify the specific facts within the text. However, they may not understand texts in which the concepts are presented in a decontextualized manner, the sentence structure is complex, or the vocabulary is abstract or has multiple meanings. They can read independently but may have occasional comprehension problems, especially when processing grade-level information.	Choose vocabulary and sentence structure based on students' comprehension; repeat and rephrase as needed; accompany oral instruction with visuals and hands-on activities. Make connections to students' prior personal and academic experiences. Ask critical thinking questions that can be answered with phrases and simple sentences. Address various learning modalities. Provide texts at students' readability level. Teach students to use glossaries and their vocabulary notes as references. Provide models and less scaffolding for writing. Assess students using Sentence Frames/Starters; follow with specific oral prompting for ambiguities.
L5: Bridging Students can express themselves fluently and spontaneously on a wide range of personal, general, academic, and social topics in a variety of contexts. They are poised to function in an environment with native-speaking peers with minimal language support or guidance. Students have a good command of technical and academic vocabulary as well as of idiomatic expressions and colloquialisms. They can produce clear, smoothly flowing, well-structured texts of differing lengths and degrees of linguistic complexity. Errors are minimal, difficult to spot, and generally corrected when they occur.	Use vocabulary and sentence structure normal for grade level. Make connections to students' prior learning. Ask critical thinking questions and encourage responses that are detailed sentences. Address various learning modalities. Provide texts at students' readability level and grade level. Provide models and minimal use of scaffolds for writing; integrate language arts and content-area activities and give feedback to continue developing language and writing skills. Assess students' independent writing; provide clear directions, writing models, and paragraph starters/outlines.

Source: The language characteristics in this table's left column come from http://www.tesol.org and are used with permission.

It may take five to seven years for an English learner to progress from the Entering ELP level to achieving academic language proficiency in reading, writing, listening, and speaking close to that of a native English speaker. English learners, like other students, are very heterogeneous, and their progress can depend on a complexity of factors, so individuals may reach proficiency in fewer than five years or more than seven years.

ACADEMIC LANGUAGE SKILLS CHARTS

The next set of figures (Figures 3.2 through 3.5) consists of Academic Language Skills charts, which provide more detailed performance indicators for English learners at each of the five proficiency levels. These indicators describe what we consider to be the language skills most essential for a student to communicate (understand and express ideas) in any core content area. Teachers can use the chart for their grade span to quickly see what to expect of English learners at each proficiency level, judge their own English learners' current levels, and consider instructional strategies appropriate to each level. The charts help teachers pinpoint where a student is for a particular language skill and then plan to differentiate lessons for teaching and assessing English learners according to their levels.

These charts show specific academic language skills at each of the five ELP levels, for grades 1–3, 4–5, 6–8, and 9–12, respectively.[5] The descriptors at each ELP level reflect mastery of that level. A newly arrived English learner who understands few or no words in English is working in the Entering level but needs developmental time to show mastery of those descriptors. The Bridging level reflects near-native English speaker proficiency. Knowing what to expect of English learners at the different ELP levels helps a teacher plan instruction that ensures English learners can access the curriculum. Scaffolding strategies are used to support learning and performance as needed at each level.

There are seven skills at grades 1–3 and 4–5 and eight skills at grades 6–8 and 9–12.[6]

One of the skills across all grade levels is "use writing strategies"; it is based on a broadly accepted writing process: prewriting, writing, responding, revising, editing, and publishing/sharing.[7] Another skill common to all grade levels, "communicate critical thinking" defines the rigor of thinking in other skills and was informed by core content area standards and Bloom's taxonomy of higher-order thinking.[8] Although all students can think critically, English learners at the lower ELP levels and some students with learning difficulties struggle to *communicate* their thinking.

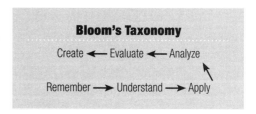

For example, the Academic Language Skills chart for grades 6–8 (Figure 3.4) shows that all English learners are expected to learn the skill of discerning the main ideas in a passage, gradually increasing communication from *identifying* a main idea at the Entering level to *explaining* main ideas by using *academic discourse* at the Bridging level. What kinds of main ideas might be addressed while avoiding dumbing down content to just basic facts? The skill "communicate critical thinking" reflects the level of rigor that students should be able to demonstrate at each ELP level. The teacher will need to scaffold learning for students at each level so they learn the same content or skill within their zone of proximal development.

Later chapters address strategies for developing academic vocabulary and discourse in a discipline and scaffolding strategies for students to learn the content of the discipline.

Teachers may have English learners in their classrooms at some or all of the five levels, and any individual student's skill level may vary, depending on whether a listening, speaking, reading, or writing skill is being assessed. The challenge for the teacher is successfully teaching grade-level concepts within a year to English learners who take many years to reach academic English proficiency. The high school English learner cannot spend many years learning English before taking courses required for college entrance. So the teachers in core disciplines must give English learners the same opportunity as native English speakers to learn the academic content of the course. To provide the same opportunity, teachers will need to use a variety of scaffolding strategies that are effective for English learners (and students with learning difficulties) — the focus of this guidebook.

The Academic Language Skills charts that follow can also be used as rubrics by an English or ELD/ESL teacher to determine the language proficiency level of an English learner at any point in time. Often the only assessment data available to these teachers are state test scores, which may be both too general and too old to help guide skill-based instruction in the present.

FIGURE 3.2. Academic Language Skills, Grades 1–3

Skill	L1: Entering	L2: Emerging	L3: Developing	L4: Expanding	L5: Bridging
Listen with Comprehension	Listen to and follow one-step directions using real-life objects, with visual cues from the teacher.	Listen to and follow one-step directions with visual cues from the teacher.	Listen to and follow two-step simple directions with visual cues from the teacher.	Listen to and follow multistep simple directions.	Listen to and follow multistep directions.
	Listen to teacher's simple questions, answers, and brief explanations, and identify basic facts using nonverbal responses and a few words orally.	Listen to teacher's simple questions, answers, and brief explanations, and orally identify a few key concepts using phrases and simple sentences (subject-verb-object).	Listen to teacher's simple questions, answers, and brief explanations, and orally identify some key concepts and some details.	Listen to teacher's simple questions, answers, and brief explanations, and orally identify key concepts and supporting details.	Listen to teacher's simple questions, answers, and brief explanations, and orally describe key concepts and supporting details.
Use Academic Vocabulary	Use some basic vocabulary to communicate needs and basic information.	Use more basic and a few academic words in phrases and simple sentences to communicate basic information.	Use more key academic words to communicate information.	Use function words to connect expanding academic vocabulary to express some complex ideas.	Use grade-appropriate academic discourse to express complex ideas in a wide variety of academic settings.
Ask and Answer Questions Orally	Ask and answer questions by using nonverbal responses or simple verbal responses.	Ask and answer factual comprehension questions by using phrases or simple sentences.	Ask and answer factual comprehension questions by using simple sentences.	Ask and answer factual comprehension questions by using sentences with some supporting details.	Ask and answer factual comprehension questions by using sentences with many supporting details.
Retell Main Ideas	Retell a few basic, familiar concepts by using nonverbal responses and a few words.	Retell literal main ideas by using verbal phrases and some simple sentences.	Retell literal and some basic abstract main ideas by using more detailed sentences.	Retell main ideas with some paraphrasing and some supporting details.	Retell main ideas with paraphrasing and supporting details.
Use Writing Strategies	Label graphic organizers with key words to express ideas or the meaning of vocabulary words.	Use labels and phrases in graphic organizers and Sentence Frames to express ideas or the meaning of vocabulary words.	Use the writing process with teacher guidance to write sentences (grade 1) or a short paragraph (grades 2–3) to express an idea.	Use the writing process more independently to write sentences (grade 1) or a paragraph (grades 2–3).	Use the writing process to write clear and connected sentences (grade 1) or brief paragraphs (grades 2–3).

FIGURE 3.2. **Academic Language Skills, Grades 1–3 (continued)**

Skill	L1: Entering	L2: Emerging	L3: Developing	L4: Expanding	L5: Bridging
Write Compositions	Copy the English alphabet legibly; write target words, perhaps with aid of Word Walls or other sources; illustrate ideas appropriately.	Use Sentence Frames to write one or two simple sentences; illustrate ideas appropriately.	Use Sentence Frames with fewer scaffolds to write simple sentences; illustrate ideas appropriately.	Use more detailed sentences in grade 1; write some connected sentences in grades 2–3.	Write a few connected sentences in grade 1; write short compositions with connected sentences in grades 2–3.
Communicate Critical Thinking	Use gestures and a few words to: » compare and contrast; » identify simple sequential or chronological order (e.g., beginning, middle, end); » identify conclusions.	Use phrases to: » compare and contrast; » recognize cause and effect relationships; » identify sequential or chronological order; » make predictions.	Use simple sentences to: » compare and contrast; » recognize cause and effect relationships; » identify sequential or chronological order; » make and confirm predictions.	Use detailed sentences to: » compare and contrast; » recognize cause and effect relationships; » identify sequential or chronological order; » make and confirm predictions.	Use a few connected sentences with details to: » compare and contrast; » recognize cause and effect relationships; » identify sequential or chronological order; » make and confirm predictions.

FIGURE 3.3. Academic Language Skills, Grades 4–5

Skill	L1: Entering	L2: Emerging	L3: Developing	L4: Expanding	L5: Bridging
Listen with Comprehension	Listen to and follow simple directions.	Listen to and follow a few complex directions.	Listen to and follow several multistep directions.	Listen to and follow multistep directions.	Listen to and follow multistep directions.
	Listen to teacher's simple questions, answers, and brief explanations, and show understanding of basic facts using gestures and oral phrases.	Listen to teacher's questions, answers, and brief explanations, and show understanding by identifying some key ideas using simple sentences orally.	Listen to teacher's questions, answers, and explanations, and show understanding by briefly describing key ideas orally.	Listen to teacher's questions, answers, and explanations, and show understanding by describing key ideas with some details orally.	Listen during teacher's lesson and engage in class discussion with only whole-class visual aids and show understanding by explaining key ideas using connected sentences orally.
Use Academic Vocabulary	Use some basic vocabulary words to communicate needs and basic information.	Use basic and a few key academic vocabulary words to communicate basic information.	Use some key academic vocabulary words and some function words to communicate information. Use context clues to understand a few unknown words.	Use function words to connect academic vocabulary to express some complex ideas. Use context clues and a glossary to understand some unknown words.	Use grade-appropriate academic discourse to express complex ideas in a wide variety of academic settings. Use context clues and a dictionary to understand many unknown words.
Ask and Answer Questions Orally	Ask and answer simple factual comprehension questions by using nonverbal or simple verbal responses.	Ask and answer factual comprehension questions by using phrases or simple sentences.	Ask and answer factual comprehension questions that require critical thinking by using some detailed sentences.	Ask and answer comprehension questions with some supporting details that require critical thinking.	Ask and answer comprehension questions with many supporting details that require critical thinking.
Describe Main Ideas	Retell familiar information and identify the main idea using nonverbal or simple verbal responses.	Retell familiar information and identify the main idea by using phrases or simple sentences.	Describe the main idea of informational materials with a few supporting details using some connected sentences.	Describe the main ideas of informational materials with supporting details in connected sentences.	Explain the main ideas of informational materials using academic discourse.

FIGURE 3.3. **Academic Language Skills, Grades 4–5 (continued)**

Skill	L1: Entering	L2: Emerging	L3: Developing	L4: Expanding	L5: Bridging
Use Writing Strategies	As a guided prewriting activity, use labels and phrases in simple graphic organizers. As a guided writing activity, use Sentence Frames to write words and brief phrases to express ideas.	As a guided prewriting activity, use a few complex graphic organizers. As a guided writing activity, use phrases in Sentence Frames and prompts for simple sentences to express ideas.	Use prewriting activities and writing activities with Sentence Starters. Use guided responding, revising, and editing to create a few paragraphs that develop a central idea.	Use all of the steps of the writing process (a second draft at the publishing stage) to write paragraphs that develop a central idea with some supporting details.	Use all of the steps of the writing process to publish clear, coherent, focused essays and reports.
Write in Content Areas	Label graphic organizers using key words and phrases. Write words and brief phrases in simple Sentence Frames.	Write phrases using simple and complex Sentence Frames. Use prompts to write simple sentences. Texts may include many errors in grammar and conventions that impede meaning.	Write sentences and brief compositions; may need Sentence Starters. Texts may include errors that impede meaning; some errors may reflect first-language interference.	Write compositions that include a main idea and some supporting details. Texts may include some inconsistent errors that may impede meaning; some errors may reflect first-language interference.	Write well-developed compositions that include a main idea and many supporting details. Texts may include a few minor errors that do not impede meaning and may be typical of native English peers.
Communicate Critical Thinking	Use gestures and a few words to: » compare and contrast; » identify simple sequential or chronological order.	Use phrases and simple sentences to: » compare and contrast; » identify sequential or chronological order; » distinguish between fact and opinion; » make predictions and draw simple conclusions.	Use sentences with some details to: » compare and contrast; » describe sequential or chronological order; » describe cause and effect relationships; » distinguish between fact and opinion; » make and confirm predictions, draw conclusions, and make generalizations.	Use a few connected sentences with details to: » compare and contrast; » analyze sequential or chronological order; » identify cause and effect relationships; » distinguish between fact and opinion; » make and confirm predictions, draw conclusions, and make inferences and generalizations.	Use academic discourse to: » compare and contrast; » analyze sequential or chronological order; » identify cause and effect relationships; » distinguish between fact and opinion; » make and confirm predictions, draw conclusions, and make inferences and generalizations.

FIGURE 3.4. Academic Language Skills, Grades 6–8

Skill	L1: Entering	L2: Emerging	L3: Developing	L4: Expanding	L5: Bridging
Listen with Comprehension	Listen to and follow simple directions.	Listen to and follow a few complex directions.	Listen to and follow several multistep directions.	Listen to and follow multistep directions.	Listen to and follow multistep directions.
	Listen to teacher's simple questions, answers, and brief explanations, and identify one or a few key ideas using gestures and oral phrases.	Listen to teacher's questions, answers, and brief explanations, and identify some key ideas using simple sentences.	Listen to teacher's questions, answers, and explanations, and describe key ideas with some details.	Listen to teacher's questions, answers, and explanations, and explain key ideas in detail.	Listen during teacher's lesson and engage in class discussion with only whole-class visual aids and explain key ideas using connected sentences.
Use Academic Vocabulary	Use basic vocabulary and a few academic vocabulary words to communicate basic information.	Use basic and a few key academic vocabulary words in phrases and simple sentences to communicate meaning. Use context clues to understand a few unknown words.	Use some key academic vocabulary words and function words to communicate information. Use glossary, knowledge of some word parts, and context to understand some unknown words. Recognize multiple meanings of some words.	Use expanding academic vocabulary and function words to express some complex ideas. Use glossary, expanding knowledge of word parts, and context to understand many unknown words. Recognize multiple meanings of many words.	Use academic discourse to express complex ideas in a wide variety of academic settings. Use knowledge of word parts and context as well as dictionary to understand unknown words. Recognize multiple meanings of many words.
Ask and Answer Questions Orally	Ask and answer simple factual comprehension questions using nonverbal or simple verbal responses.	Ask and answer factual comprehension questions using phrases or simple sentences.	Ask and answer factual comprehension questions that require critical thinking, using some detailed sentences.	Ask and answer factual comprehension questions with some supporting details that require critical thinking.	Ask and answer factual comprehension questions with many supporting details that require critical thinking.
Explain Main Ideas	Orally identify a main idea and a few details in informational materials by using nonverbal or simple verbal responses.	Orally describe a main idea and some details in informational materials by using phrases and simple sentences.	Orally explain the main ideas and some supporting details in informational materials by using some connected sentences.	Explain the main ideas with supporting details in informational materials by using connected sentences.	Explain the main ideas in informational materials by using academic discourse.

FIGURE 3.4. **Academic Language Skills, Grades 6–8 (continued)**

Skill	L1: Entering	L2: Emerging	L3: Developing	L4: Expanding	L5: Bridging
Use Writing Strategies	As a guided prewriting activity, fill in simple graphic organizers. As a guided writing activity, use Sentence Frames, pictures, lists, charts, and tables to express ideas.	As a prewriting activity, use a few complex graphic organizers. As a writing activity, use prompts, Sentence Frames, pictures, lists, charts, and tables to create a brief paragraph that expresses ideas.	Use prewriting activities, including note taking and outlining, and writing activities with Sentence Starters. Use guided responding, revising, and editing to create brief essays or reports that develop a central idea.	Use all of the steps of the writing process (a second draft at the publishing stage) to write paragraphs in focused essays or reports that develop a central idea with some supporting details.	Use all of the steps of the writing process to publish clear, coherent, focused essays and reports.
Write Compositions	Label graphic organizers using key words and phrases. Write words, phrases, and simple sentences by using Sentence Frames.	Write brief, simple compositions that include a main idea and some details by using Sentence Frames. Texts may include many errors in grammar and conventions that impede meaning.	Write brief compositions that include a thesis and some supporting details. Texts may include errors that impede meaning; some errors may reflect first-language interference.	Write compositions that include a clear thesis and supporting details. Texts may include some inconsistent errors that may impede meaning; some errors may reflect first-language interference.	Write well-developed compositions that include a clear thesis and supporting details. Texts may include a few minor errors that do not impede meaning and may be typical of native English peers.
Write Research Reports	Gather basic information as part of a group. Present information graphically with labels and write simple sentences by using Sentence Frames.	Gather some complex information as part of a group. Present information graphically and write brief summary paragraphs by using Sentence Frames. Texts may include many errors that impede meaning.	Investigate a topic as part of a group. Develop a brief report that includes source citations. Texts may include errors that impede meaning.	Investigate a topic and write a full report that conveys information; use technical terms, citations, and a bibliography. Texts may include some inconsistent errors that may impede meaning.	Investigate and write reports that clarify and defend positions with evidence and logical reasoning; use technical terms, citations, and a bibliography. Texts may include a few minor errors that do not impede meaning.
Communicate Critical Thinking	Use nonverbal communication and words or phrases to: » compare and contrast; » identify cause and effect and sequential order relationships; » identify facts and opinions.	Use phrases and simple sentences to: » compare and contrast; » identify cause and effect and sequential order relationships; » distinguish between fact and opinion; » hypothesize and conclude.	Use sentences with some details to: » compare and contrast; » describe cause and effect and sequential order relationships; » distinguish between fact and opinion; » hypothesize, conclude, and generalize.	Use connected sentences with details to: » compare and contrast; » analyze various relationships; » distinguish among fact, opinion, and supported inferences; » hypothesize, conclude, and generalize.	Use academic discourse to: » compare and contrast; » analyze various relationships; » identify relative credibility of information; » hypothesize, conclude, and generalize.

FIGURE 3.5. **Academic Language Skills, Grades 9–12**

Skill	L1: Entering	L2: Emerging	L3: Developing	L4: Expanding	L5: Bridging
Listen with Comprehension	Listen to and follow simple directions.	Listen to and follow a few complex directions.	Listen to and follow several multistep directions.	Listen to and follow multistep directions.	Listen to and follow multistep directions.
	Listen to teacher's simple questions, answers, and brief explanations, and identify one or a few key ideas using gestures and oral phrases.	Listen to teacher's questions, answers, and brief explanations, and identify some key ideas using simple sentences.	Listen to teacher's questions, answers, and explanations, and describe key ideas with some details.	Listen to teacher's questions, answers, and explanations, and explain key ideas in detail.	Listen during teacher's lesson and engage in class discussion with only whole-class visual aids and explain key ideas using connected sentences.
Use Academic Vocabulary	Use basic vocabulary and a few academic vocabulary words to communicate basic information.	Use basic and some key academic vocabulary words in phrases and simple sentences to communicate meaning. Use context clues to understand a few unknown words.	Use key academic vocabulary words and function words to communicate information. Use glossary, knowledge of some word parts, and context to understand some unknown words. Recognize multiple meanings of some words.	Use expanding academic vocabulary and function words to express some complex ideas. Use glossary, expanding knowledge of word parts, and context to understand many unknown words. Recognize multiple meanings of many words.	Use academic discourse to express complex ideas in a wide variety of academic settings. Use knowledge of word parts and context as well as dictionary to understand unknown words. Recognize multiple meanings of many words.
Ask and Answer Questions Orally	Ask and answer simple factual comprehension questions using nonverbal or simple verbal responses.	Ask and answer factual comprehension questions using phrases or simple sentences.	Ask and answer factual comprehension questions that require critical thinking, using some detailed sentences.	Ask and answer factual comprehension questions with some supporting details that require critical thinking.	Ask and answer factual comprehension questions with many supporting details that require critical thinking.
Analyze Main Ideas	Orally identify a main idea and a few details in informational materials by using nonverbal or simple verbal responses.	Orally describe a main idea and some details in informational materials by using some connected sentences.	Orally explain the main ideas and some supporting details in informational materials by using connected sentences.	Analyze the main ideas by connecting important details in informational materials by using several paragraphs.	Analyze the main ideas in informational materials by using academic discourse.

FIGURE 3.5. **Academic Language Skills, Grades 9–12 (continued)**

Skill	L1: Entering	L2: Emerging	L3: Developing	L4: Expanding	L5: Bridging
Use Writing Strategies	As a guided prewriting activity, fill in simple graphic organizers. As a guided writing activity, use Sentence Frames, pictures, lists, charts, and tables to express ideas.	As a prewriting activity, use complex graphic organizers. As a writing activity, use prompts, Sentence Frames, pictures, lists, charts, and tables to create a brief paragraph that expresses ideas.	Use prewriting activities, including note taking and outlining, and writing activities with Sentence Starters. Use guided responding, revising, and editing to create brief essays or reports that develop a central idea.	Use all of the steps of the writing process (a second draft at the publishing stage) to write paragraphs in focused essays or reports that develop a central idea with some supporting details.	Use all of the steps of the writing process to publish clear, coherent, focused essays and reports.
Write Compositions	Label graphic organizers using key words and phrases. Write words, phrases, and simple sentences by using Sentence Frames.	Write brief, simple compositions that include a main idea and some details by using Sentence Frames. Texts may include many errors in grammar and conventions that impede meaning.	Write brief compositions that include a thesis and some supporting details. Texts may include errors that impede meaning; some errors may reflect first-language interference.	Write compositions that include a clear thesis and describe supporting details. Texts may include some inconsistent errors that may impede meaning; some errors may reflect first-language interference.	Write well-developed compositions that include a clear thesis and organized, supporting details. Texts may include a few minor errors that do not impede meaning and may be typical of native English peers.
Write Research Reports	Gather basic information as part of a group. Present information graphically with labels and write simple sentences by using Sentence Frames.	Gather some complex information as part of a group. Present information graphically and write brief summary paragraphs by using Sentence Frames. Texts may include many errors that impede meaning.	Investigate a topic as part of a group. Develop a brief report that includes source citations. Texts may include errors that impede meaning.	Investigate a topic and write a full report that conveys information; use technical terms, citations, and a bibliography. Texts may include some inconsistent errors that may impede meaning.	Investigate and write reports that clarify and defend positions with evidence and logical reasoning; use technical terms, citations, and a bibliography. Texts may include a few minor errors that do not impede meaning.
Communicate Critical Thinking	Use nonverbal communication and words or phrases to: » compare and contrast; » identify cause and effect and sequential order relationships; » identify facts and opinions.	Use phrases and simple sentences to: » compare and contrast; » identify cause and effect and sequential order relationships; » distinguish between fact and opinion; » hypothesize and conclude.	Use sentences with some details to: » compare and contrast; » describe cause and effect and sequential order relationships; » distinguish between fact and opinion; » hypothesize, conclude, and generalize.	Use connected sentences with details to: » compare and contrast; » analyze various relationships; » distinguish among fact, opinion, and supported inferences; » hypothesize, conclude, and generalize.	Use academic discourse to: » compare and contrast; » analyze various relationships; » identify relative credibility of information; » hypothesize, conclude, and generalize.

ENGLISH LEARNERS WHO ALSO HAVE LEARNING DIFFICULTIES

Teachers need to be aware that some English learners have the additional characteristic of having learning difficulties. These students have the double challenge of learning a new language while also having receptive and expressive language difficulties. Language overload can be exhausting for any English learner and especially so for students with difficulties in auditory language processing, working memory processing, or language expression. The novice English learner with a learning difficulty may quickly become exhausted while processing the teacher's question in English, thinking of an answer in his or her primary language or in English or a combination, and trying to express an answer in English using correct grammatical structures.

Normally, when an English learner has acquired enough English, certain structures are automatized, so the student just knows — without thinking about English language rules — what is the correct phrase or sentence structure to express an idea. However, particularly for students whose native language is very different from English, such automatizing can take a long time. Thai, for example, is very different from English in that *he* or *she* can be the same word, the verb does not need to be changed for subject-verb agreement, and past and future tenses are denoted by pairing a present tense verb with a "helper" word denoting time. An English learner from Thailand might say "He see car" instead of "She saw the car" when referring to Mary and what happened in the past, and other students may laugh, thinking the English learner cannot differentiate genders. Also, the Thai language does not have articles, so knowing the difference between *the* and *a/an* and remembering to use the appropriate article is yet another challenge when speaking or writing. For students who have expressive language difficulties, it may be that they struggle to speak or write an idea because they have difficulty forming memories of language structures so they can be automatically retrieved, and this is exacerbated for an English learner with sparse English vocabulary and difficulty with native language automaticity.

The best we can posit at this time is that the reason an English learner with a learning difficulty is not making expected English language progress is because the student may be challenged to form memories of language structures so they become automatic in use. (See the accompanying vignette — "Listening with Understanding" — for a brief example of another kind of miscommunication that can occur with a student who is both an English learner and has learning difficulties.)

Determining why a student is not making progress or little progress is complicated and requires an individualized approach that is led by a team of qualified members, including members who know and understand the individual well in order to make appropriate decisions beyond universal screening and progress monitoring data.

LISTENING WITH UNDERSTANDING

Natthaphon was born in Thailand where he did not speak more than a word to express himself until he was 3 years old. It was suspected that he had a language disability and autism. At 5 years of age, he immigrated to the United States, and he was given the nickname Tony because it was much easier for Americans to read and pronounce. Nicknames are common in Thai culture, and he knew the nickname he had in Thailand. In the United States, he learned to write "Tony" on work papers in kindergarten.

On his first day in first grade, his homework assignment was to practice writing his *full* name. He wrote, "Tony table 1."

Why did he not write his actual last name? Tony's kindergarten teacher said that every time he got out of his seat and wandered around the room, she would point to his seat and say, "Tony, table 1." Although she intended simply to tell him to return to his designated seat, Tony thought she was saying his whole name as she pointed to where he should sit.

Guided by the indicator for "Listen with Understanding" in the grades 1–3 academic language skills chart (Figure 3.2), the teacher could have improved her communication with Tony by giving him a one-step direction, a full but simple sentence with more meaningful visual cues. She would not need to dumb down her English command, but instead could model a simple sentence.

For example, she might have walked over to Tony and said, "Tony, please go sit at table 1" while motioning him toward the table with a gentle hand on his shoulder. A lesson on following simple directions, such as "stand up" and "sit down," in which Tony and other students kinesthetically respond to various directions also would help all students' vocabulary development and could have helped avoid the humorous but unfortunate miscommunication that Tony and the teacher experienced.

ENDNOTES FOR CHAPTER 3

[1] Short, D. J., & Fitzsimmons, S. (2007). *Double the work: Challenges and solutions to acquiring language and academic literacy for adolescent English language learners.* New York: Alliance for Excellent Education.

[2] Vygotsky, L. (1962). *Thought and language.* Cambridge, MA: MIT Press. See p. 108.

[3] Title III of the federal No Child Left Behind Act mentions ELD and ELP levels interchangeably and the labels "beginning, early intermediate, intermediate, early advanced, and advanced" for the performance levels. California (as of January 2011) uses the term *ELD levels* and the Title III labels. California's terminology was used in the two previous guidebooks coauthored by John Carr for science and mathematics teachers — Carr, J., Sexton, U., & Lagunoff, R. (2007). *Making science accessible to English learners: A guidebook for teachers.* San Francisco: WestEd; Carr, J., Carroll, C., Cremer, S., Gale, M., Lagunoff, R., & Sexton, U. (2009). *Making mathematics accessible to English learners: A guidebook for teachers.* San Francisco: WestEd. This guidebook uses terminology that reflects language found in World-Class Instructional Design and Assessment (WIDA) and Teachers of English to Speakers of Other Languages (TESOL) standards.

[4] Many states have adopted or adapted the WIDA ELP standards. WIDA's 2012 draft edition substitutes "Entering" for "Starting" as the first ELP level, among other enhancements. These performance indicators are based on WIDA/TESOL

ELP standards that are now aligned with the Common Core English Language Arts standards. For more information on WIDA and TESOL ELP standards, see the WIDA website http://www.wida.us/standards/elp.aspx and the TESOL website http://www.tesol.org/s_tesol/seccss.asp?CID=86&DID=1556

[5] Carr, J., Sexton, U., & Lagunoff, R. (2007). See Chapter 3; Carr, J., Carroll, C., Cremer, S., Gale, M., Lagunoff, R., & Sexton, U. (2009). See Chapter 3.

[6] Carr, J., Sexton, U., & Lagunoff, R. (2007). See Chapter 3.

[7] One of many online resources describing the writing process is http://faculty.uoit.ca/hughes/Writing/WritingProcess.html

[8] Anderson, L. W., & Krathwohl, D. R. (Eds.). (2001). *A taxonomy for learning, teaching and assessing: A revision of Bloom's Taxonomy of educational objectives.* New York: Longman. See pp. 67–68.

CHAPTER 4

Teaching and Using Academic Language

> **I think in pictures. Words are like a second language to me. I translate both spoken and written words into full-color movies, complete with sound.**
>
> — Temple Grandin

Much of what students need to learn in any discipline requires that they master specialized vocabulary and discipline-specific ways of using language, whether for listening, speaking, reading, or writing. Integrating language instruction into content instruction is a research-based approach that works, and effective teachers do this for all their students.[1] Integrating language and content instruction accelerates English language development, shortens the delay before English learners and students with certain learning difficulties have equitable access to content curriculum, and supports culturally and linguistically inclusive classrooms.[2] For English learners and students with language difficulties, learning language in the context of learning content is not simply beneficial, it is crucial.[3] Language learning and content learning are inseparable — and reciprocal.[4]

This chapter describes the teacher's role in facilitating students' language use and presents some concrete steps for teaching new vocabulary. Then a number of tools are introduced that teachers can use to help students organize concepts and vocabulary. Teachers should keep in mind that the language objective is not limited to word/term definitions but extends to the appropriate use of academic words and terms as they are embedded in oral or written language to clearly and effectively communicate ideas in the style of a mathematician, political speech writer, scientist, or historian, to name a few careers that learners might choose to pursue.

THE LEXICON AND DISCOURSE OF A DISCIPLINE

Academic language that relates specifically to a discipline is the *lexicon of the discipline* — the set of terms professionals in the discipline and students of the discipline use to communicate about their subject matter. These content words and phrases have a specific meaning in the context of the discipline. It is important to explicitly teach English learners and students with learning difficulties (particularly language difficulties) the words and terms that have multiple meanings across disciplines.

As a very simple example, consider the common function or transition word *by*. *Merriam-Webster's Collegiate Dictionary, 11th ed.*, offers 11 definitions. When hearing the teacher say the word, the English learner or student with learning difficulties might be thinking *bi* or *buy* and be quite confused. In language arts, *by* can mean *in proximity* (e.g., "he stood by the barn"), *through the agency of* (e.g., "written by Shakespeare"), or many other meanings. In mathematics, *by* is a function word in multiplication (e.g., "multiple 2 by 3"), division (e.g., "divide 10 by 2"), and measurement (e.g., "the room is 10' by 12'"). In social science, *by* can mean *not later than* (e.g., "Name the states that were admitted into the union by 1803").

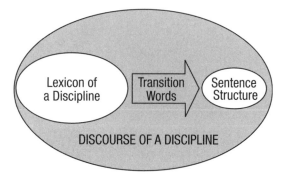

A similar challenge for English learners and students with certain learning difficulties is that sometimes several different words can describe the same thing. For example, *add*, *plus*, and *sum* all refer to the same mathematical operation.[5] Examples of terms that have specific meanings in mathematics and are clearly part of the lexicon are *quadratic*, *algebraic*, *quotient*, and *square root*. Terms such as *difference* and *evaluate* have different meanings in other disciplines. *Difference* means the answer to a subtraction operation in mathematics, but in science it refers to a quality that is not the same about two items. In mathematics, to *evaluate* an equation means to find the values that make the equation true. In the social sciences, to *evaluate* a source means to rate the quality or veracity of the source. Some everyday words have a specific meaning in a mathematics context (e.g., *positive*, *negative*, *table*, *rational*, *irrational*) but may have different meanings in language arts, science, or social science. In biology, words such as *conservative*, *translation*, and *replication* have different meanings than in other disciplines.

Words are embedded in sentences (brief discourse), which are connected in paragraphs (longer discourse) to communicate complex concepts and interrelationships. The style or pattern of written discourse, how ideas are conveyed, can differ significantly among disciplines. Struggling readers, English learners, and students with learning difficulties may need explicit instruction about how to read text in each discipline to find information such as key word definitions, examples and nonexamples, and supporting details. When the lexicon of a discipline is used in sentences, further comprehension challenges arise. National Council of Teachers of Mathematics standards as well as research on the language of mathematics, for example, point out that mathematics discourse patterns and syntactical structures can be daunting for English learners to understand and use.[6,7] And students with learning difficulties can face difficulty organizing and holding a complex idea in working memory long enough to find and coherently express the idea in words. A novel might start with a current event and then go back in time to describe the past cause of a current effect, and another novel might start by presenting details about a character or event that much later in the story become clues to a cause and effect or problem and resolution.

Active voice sentences tend to be easier to comprehend than passive voice sentences, but text and speech often use passive voice (e.g., "10 divided by 2"; "Abraham Lincoln was shot by John Wilkes Booth"). Moreover, academic texts often lack the redundancy or paraphrasing that assists English learners in understanding the text, and for some English learners and students with learning difficulties, sentence structures can be too complex to comprehend. Also, passive voice and sentence structures in academic texts can make reading with comprehension difficult for some students with learning difficulties. Although an author may define a key term in one sentence and then use a function word to start the next sentence to help the student make a comparison or contrast, that function word may be unknown to an English learner or may overwhelm the student with a learning difficulty who has trouble keeping all of the information in working memory and abstractly creating a connection between the two sentences. Also, English language arts Common Core state standards include interpreting charts, graphs, and tables in multimedia formats. The student who is an English learner and has a learning difficulty may become completely confused by trying to make sense of so many sources at once.

The language of mathematics can be particularly challenging, as mathematics statements can be expressed entirely in symbols or in very technical language. In symbolic vocabulary, for example, the numeral *2* has very different meanings in each of the following contexts: 52, 23, 4^2, 1/2, 2/3, 2n.[8] The notation 5^2 can be read as "five squared," "five to the second power," or "five to the second."[9] Often, there is no direct correspondence between how symbols and words are ordered (e.g., "*a* is five less than *b*" means "*a* = *b* – 5," not "*a* = 5 – *b*").[10] English learners who try to translate word-for-word may have difficulty interpreting the meaning of logical connectors such as *if, because,* and *however.*[11] In addition, within mathematics, notational and procedural differences exist between the United States and other countries, such as the use of a period (".") versus a comma (",").

Figure 4.1 lists commonly used function words and phrases that English learners and students with learning difficulties need to understand. We encourage teachers to post a chart like this on the wall and give a copy to students to keep. Students must learn and practice using the function words, so teachers must identify key words/phrases that are new to students and teach them by front-loading instruction before teaching content in a manner that assumes all students know the function words. One way to do this is by giving students examples of the words used in contexts with low cognitive load, contexts in which the content is familiar to students so they can focus on the function words that are new to them. Student groups might generate examples for assigned function words, get whole-class (and teacher) agreement that the examples are appropriate, and post the full set on the wall or put it in students' notebooks. The teacher can differentiate this task by matching the difficulty level of function words to the proficiency levels of groups.

FIGURE 4.1. Common Function Words

Many function words or phrases can be used as Sentences Starters, and some connect ideas inside a sentence.

Purpose	Transition Words			
Giving a definition	is equal to	means	refers to	is synonymous with
	is the same as	in other words	consists of	
Providing an example	for example	for instance	such as	is like
	including	to illustrate		
Suggesting more ideas	also	finally	another	moreover
Sequencing	first ... second	next	initially	before
	preceding	when	finally	after
	following	not long after	now	
Comparing	same as	just like/as	in the same way	in comparison
	not only ... but also	as well as	similarly	
Contrasting	different from	as opposed to	instead of	in contrast
	however	but	although	yet
	while	on the other hand		
Showing cause and effect relationships	because	as a result of	may be due to	since
	consequently	this led to	so that	nevertheless
	in order to	effects of	for this reason	if ... then
	therefore	thus		
Describing problems and solutions	one answer is	one reason is	a solution is	the problem is
	the question is			
Expressing an opinion or conclusion	I think	I believe that	I predict that	I suggest that
	I conclude that	I deduce that	I speculate that	in my opinion
	I agree with ____ that			
Reporting findings or outcomes	I/We found that	I/We learned that	I/We discovered that	I/We observed that

Source: Adapted from a table developed by Pamela Spycher for WestEd's English Language and Literacy Acceleration project and used with permission from Pamela Spycher.

To become familiar with the lexicon of a discipline, English learners need to practice using it in sentences and extended discourse. Sentence structure governs the formation of sentences — the combining of content and transition words into statements, questions, and commands. At a level beyond the sentence, discourse involves use of language to convey extended expression of thought on a topic in connected speech or writing. A key aspect of the discourse of a discipline is communication about its procedures — for example, knowing how to provide a solution supported by mathematical reasoning; how to write a summary or explanation of a science investigation; or how to present arguments and supporting details for social science or language arts (e.g., persuasive essay, research paper).

FACILITATING STUDENTS' LANGUAGE USE

English learners and students with learning difficulties can learn the lexicon and discourse of a discipline. However, as we saw in chapters 2 and 3, the complexity of the language components that students can handle will vary according to students' English language proficiency. So all students can learn the same concepts, but the teacher needs to adjust the complexity of language he or she uses to explain these concepts depending on each student's language proficiency level.

The teacher also needs to support all diverse learners with hands-on activities and visuals. Visuals might be real objects, pictures, illustrations, graphic organizers, Word Walls, or board notes (see chapter 5 for more on a variety of visuals that can be used). The teacher should repeat and rephrase for English learners and provide adequate wait time (five to seven seconds) before asking for responses to accommodate English learners and students with learning difficulties who need more time to process information. Wait time encourages deeper thinking and equalizes students' opportunities to think and respond.

A student with autism spectrum disorder may say too little or too much in response to a question because the student does not realize how much is appropriate in a particular context. A speech therapist can help such a student learn to use appropriate questions or answers during social and academic conversations. A general education teacher might guide a student with ASD who responds in too few words with prompts such as, "Tell me a little more about …," "Why do you think that …," or "Can you make a sentence from what you just said?" The student also may refer to Sentence Frames, perhaps posted on the wall, to scaffold forming declarative, exclamatory, imperative, and interrogative sentences.

English learners and some students with learning difficulties may respond orally with language convention errors, such as grammatical errors or partial meanings (e.g., saying "He …" when it is ambiguous to the listener who "he" is). A teacher may implicitly correct the student's grammar by modeling the correct grammar as part of a natural response without requiring that the student repeat what was said. This may often be appropriate for the very novice English learner. As the English learner advances in vocabulary and skills, the teacher should shift to explicitly correcting errors, modeling the correct form, and asking the student to repeat back. Usually, the student will naturally repeat what was said. Again, there may be times when the teacher feels it is inappropriate to explicitly correct the student for a variety of reasons. Overtly correcting the student can raise anxiety about responding in the future, and for disciplines other than language arts, it can detract from the focus on communicating about the content of the discipline. There may be some situations when the teacher should simply ignore grammar errors; correcting all students all of the time detracts from the content area lesson, and students become anxious about grammatical correctness. Also, it's normal for anyone to make some mistakes when speaking; even a college professor giving a practiced lecture will make errors and say awkward or partial sentences.[12] By being strategic about when to address errors and whether to do so explicitly or implicitly, the teacher increases the effectiveness of the feedback that is offered.

But if the teacher never provides corrective feedback, students may likely assume that what they said was correct and needs no improvement. The same is true for writing. In many situations, the teacher can provide corrective feedback that focuses first on ideas and meaning, especially when the student is struggling to communicate complex concepts. Feedback in these instances takes the form of rephrasing by the teacher so the student hears correct grammar, as exemplified in Figure 4.2 (which provides an example of *implicit* feedback) and Figure 4.3 (which has both *implicit* and *explicit* feedback). The teacher might emphasize a target word (pause just before or after, or say the word slightly louder or slower). Also, when the teacher rephrases to correct errors and/or to provide complete information in the statement, English learners and students with learning difficulties have the opportunity they often need to hear something again in a slightly different way.

FIGURE 4.2. Example of Using Corrective Feedback

Tony asks, "Did you saw the news last night about a earthquake and tsunami in Japan?" Using implicit corrective feedback, Tony's teacher continues the conversation, "Yes, I did see news on TV about the earthquake and tsunami in Japan. What did you see about these events?"

During interactions that have a low cognitive demand, when the concept is simple or the answer is easy, the teacher should provide corrective feedback. Corrective feedback in such instances can be implicit by rephrasing a student's comment in a grammatically correct way.

FIGURE 4.3. Example of Using Corrective Feedback for Academic Language

A language objective for a science lesson is to use the word *observe* in a sentence.

Tony says, "My group saw Diet Pepsi explode when we put Mentos® in the bottle."

The teacher asks, "Did it *explode* like a bomb or *erupt* like a volcano?"

Tony replies, "It erupt."

The teacher implicitly corrects him, saying, "Yes, it erupted" as she writes the term *erupt* on a list of key terms for the whole class to see.

To provide explicit feedback, the teacher says, "Instead of *saw*, try using today's scientific word *observe*."

Tony says, "My group observe the soda erupt."

The teacher provides implicit feedback on verb tense, saying, "Yes, your group *observed* the soda erupt," and she writes this on the board.

English learners often recognize and acknowledge the corrective feedback by using the corrected word or phrase. Corrective feedback, whether in the form of rephrasing or just changing errors, is a natural and unthreatening aspect of learning in classrooms where a safe climate has been established. Students understand that the teacher will not embarrass them and their classmates will not ridicule them. Figure 4.3 presents a situation in which the teacher provides both implicit and explicit corrective feedback, knowing it will not be embarrassing for this student and it will guide other students in the class "to talk like a scientist."

English learners, particularly those below the Progressing language level, may be unsure about the meaning and use of transition words (see Figure 4.1). They may also lack the general language skills needed to discuss ideas, such as asking a clarifying question or agreeing or disagreeing with someone's idea. Figure 4.4 presents discussion Sentence Starters that can be enlarged and placed on laminated placards to post on the wall or hang from the ceiling. These Sentence Starters can help English learners to begin expressing their ideas using common words or phrases not yet in their repertoire. The Sentence Starters also help students with language difficulties to verbalize their ideas or questions. Some teachers have remarked that they have other students who also benefit from the Sentence Starters, particularly those about disagreeing or adding an idea respectfully.

TEACHING VOCABULARY

Whether in science, mathematics, social science, or other disciplines, a high percentage of the content to be taught is essentially new vocabulary words and phrases. In each discipline, students are expected to think critically and perform research and investigations. But to demonstrate that they can do these things, students must use language — they must be able to say or write responses to show their ability to meet the standards of the discipline. Therefore, even teachers who are *not* language arts specialists need to know how to help learners build their vocabularies and discourse repertoires. The strategies in this chapter are intended for just this purpose and can be used in any discipline on a frequent basis.

Many academic texts highlight key vocabulary words that are critical for understanding the topic and that many students typically will not know.[13] In addition, English learners and students with learning difficulties may not know many other words in the text that will be crucial for their full understanding of the topic. Teachers who have observed and noted the language proficiency and backgrounds of their students will be able to strategically select and teach the key words that all their students need to know, in particular their English learners and students with learning difficulties.

"High leverage" vocabulary consists of words and terms that are common to language arts, mathematics, science, and social studies. They may have the same meaning across disciplines or may have multiple meanings. A goal of vocabulary development is knowing the multiple meanings of words and using the correct meaning in a specific context. Spending time on the multiple meanings of cross-disciplinary vocabulary is important for English learners. Spending time on generalizing and recognizing different contexts for word usage is important for many students with learning difficulties, particularly those with Asperger syndrome. Vocabulary must be used many times to make it into long-term memory and become part of a student's repertoire when listening, speaking, reading, and writing. Some states have compiled lists of discipline-specific vocabulary based on the state's content standards.

FIGURE 4.4. Discussion Sentence Starters

Predicting
» I guess/predict/imagine that …

» Based on …, I infer that …

» I hypothesize that …

Expressing an Opinion
» I think/believe that …

» In my opinion …

» It seems to me that …

» Based on my experience, I think …

Asking for Clarification
» What do you mean?

» Will you explain that again?

» How did you find your answer?

Paraphrasing
» So you are saying that …

» In other words, you think …

» What I hear you saying is …

Soliciting a Response
» What do you think?

» We haven't heard from you yet.

» Do you agree?

» What is your solution? How did you get it?

Acknowledging Ideas
» My idea is similar to/related to ___'s idea.

» I agree with ___ that …

» My idea builds upon ___'s idea.

Affirming
» That's an interesting idea.

» I hadn't thought of that.

» I see what you mean.

Holding the Floor
» As I was saying, …

» If I could finish my thought, …

» What I was trying to say was …

Reporting a Partner's Idea
___ shared with me that …

___ pointed out to me that …

___ emphasized that …

___ concluded that …

Reporting a Group's Idea
We decided/agreed that …

We concluded that …

Our group sees it differently.

We had a different approach.

Disagreeing
I don't agree with you because …

I got a different answer than you.

I see it another way. I think …

Offering a Suggestion
Maybe we could …

What if we …

Here's something we might try.

Source: Adapted from *Language Strategies for Active Classroom Participation* (June 2007) with permission from Kate Kinsella. The document can be accessed as LanguageClassDiscussion.doc at http://www.sccoe.org/depts/ell/kinsella.asp. This web page also lists many other "open access" documents that Kinsella presents in her workshops.

To support English learners and students with learning difficulties, teachers need to be very deliberate about the vocabulary they choose to teach and when to teach it. Supporting the development of students' vocabulary should be done within the context of learning concepts and skills, not in isolation. Teachers should plan activities that target key vocabulary development at key points in the lesson for a section or chapter or story/book.[14] For example, an English learner at the Entering English language proficiency level may need to learn the words *egg, adult,* and *cycle* before the teacher starts a science lesson about metamorphosis, whereas other students in the class are likely to be familiar with these words. When teaching the lesson to the full class, the teacher may introduce the less familiar key words, *larva* and *pupa,* to all students by placing the words with associated pictures in a graphic organizer representing a cycle. This combination of saying and showing will help English learners, students with learning difficulties, and other primarily visual-spatial learners to understand the vocabulary words and their connections. The teacher could further support the students' language learning by having small groups listen to, speak, read, and write the words within a meaningful activity. Such repeated use of the words helps students consolidate them in long-term memory.[15]

The teacher can plan to introduce new words at the appropriate point in the lesson and repeatedly apply these new words when students speak, read, and write. For example, new vocabulary can be introduced and applied in the *engage* stage (of the 5 Es model) while connecting to prior knowledge (students' experiences or previous lessons) — this is called "front-loading" vocabulary when it is taught before the main content of the lesson. More often in disciplines other than language arts, it is appropriate to introduce new vocabulary in the *explore or explain* stages while immersed in learning the content. We contend that front-loading vocabulary is more important before reading a text (e.g., a story) in a language arts lesson than in a science, mathematics, or history lesson. For a story, front-loading helps students read with more comprehension. For a science text, on the other hand, introducing the key terms with definitions in isolation of rich context (during the lesson proper) would be ineffective. However, a teacher might ask student groups to attempt informal definitions or examples, based on what they already know, as part of the *engage* stage for the purpose of alerting students about key terms they will learn and establishing a foundation of what they already know, which can help the teacher with lesson planning.

Five Steps for Planning to Teach Vocabulary

To plan a lesson that includes explicit attention to teaching vocabulary, the teacher starts by choosing the key words in the text that students, particularly English learners, are unlikely to know; the teacher then identifies which words are most important, targets when to teach these words (during which stage of instruction), and determines how to ensure ample time to teach these words. Most key words will be discipline-specific terms, but some may be function words that connect ideas within or across sentences (e.g., *and, but, if ... then*), and some may be adjectives or adverbs that enrich the meaning of discipline-specific terms.

FIGURE 4.5. Five Steps for Planning to Teach Vocabulary

Step 1. Identify words all students need to know.

Step 2. Identify words English learners and students with learning difficulties need to know.

Step 3. Select the highest-priority words.

Step 4. Build from informal to formal understanding.

Step 5. Plan many opportunities to apply key words.

STEP 1. IDENTIFY WORDS ALL STUDENTS NEED TO KNOW

Determine which words and terms all students need to know for a lesson. For a story students will read in language arts, the words will be key to comprehending main ideas or key to a literacy skill to be taught (e.g., *cite, theme, compare and contrast, analyze, point of view*). For other disciplines, identify the key words in texts students will read or skills they will learn. The course text and content standards are the two main sources to identify these words/terms.

STEP 2. IDENTIFY WORDS ENGLISH LEARNERS AND STUDENTS WITH LEARNING DIFFICULTIES NEED TO KNOW

Search for other words in the lesson that might be new or not sufficiently understood by English learners, students with learning difficulties, and/or certain other students. English learners must be able to comprehend these key words when reading the text, interpreting a problem-solving situation, listening to teacher talk, and engaging in class discussions. These key words may be function words/phrases (see Figure 4.1).

STEP 3. SELECT THE HIGHEST-PRIORITY WORDS

After identifying key words in steps 1 and 2, it is likely there are too many words to teach in a day's lesson. Select the highest-priority words for the day's lesson and distribute other words to other days' lessons in the series on a particular topic. The highest-priority words are those which:

» are absolutely essential to understanding the lesson;

» should not be replaced with more common words (sometimes referred to as Tier One words) because they are key academic terms (known as domain-specific words) that are addressed in the Common Core Standards (e.g., *parabola* should not be replaced with *curved line*);[16,17] and

» are key words, or what Susana Dutro and Carol Moran call the "brick and mortar" words (with "bricks" being the discipline concepts and "mortar" being the function words that connect the concepts; see example in Figure 4.6).[18]

As a rule of thumb, teach no more than 8 to 10 words in a week for words that require intentional and explicit instruction, and be aware that students may learn about 2,600 other words through incidental learning.[19] The specific amount of academic vocabulary words to teach depends on each individual learner; however, it is critical that the targeted word list includes domain-specific words to prepare students to be college and career ready as addressed in the Common Core Standards for Literacy in English Language Arts and Literacy in History/Social Studies, Science, and Technical Subjects. In the content classes at the secondary level, in which students are learning multiple words in every class, teachers are encouraged to collaborate to identify the essential vocabulary words to learn. Also, English learners who know a concept in their native language and only need the translated English word(s) will need much less time to learn these words compared with learning new words for new concepts. Some of these known words may be *cognates* — words that have the same meaning and the same or similar spellings because they derive from the same ancestor language — or words one language has borrowed from the other.[20]

To judge how many words to introduce, consider what you know about your students and what words they know or likely know, how difficult the new words are, and the need to maintain the focus of instruction on the course content. It may be that some words that don't make the cut are related to higher-priority words and can be linked to them (e.g., *ratio* is related to *fraction*). Other, lower-priority words might be defined in context or simply replaced with known words to make a sentence comprehensible and allow understanding of the concept to build.

STEP 4. BUILD FROM INFORMAL TO FORMAL UNDERSTANDING

Consider whether to introduce new words before, while, or after covering a concept, keeping in mind that learning new words naturally progresses from informal to formal understanding.[21] Typically new words should be introduced in context during the lesson. Informally, start with students' own definitions, explanations, examples, or drawings for a new concept. This might occur during the *engage* stage. Then, in the *explore* or *explain* stage, you can more formally associate new words with the concept.

Activating students' prior experiences or knowledge can inform you about what students need and how to help guide their learning. Students' responses may be incomplete or very general at first; you can gradually instruct them in a word's multiple meanings or more specific meanings. Also be sure to show students how to use context clues to determine the meaning of a word. Students can keep glossaries and look up definitions in dictionaries later in a more formal process of building understanding.[22]

Students should have key terms readily available, whether posted on the classroom wall or written in notebooks or personal glossaries in which they continually enter new words, brief definitions, and other cognitive supports, such as illustrations and diagrams. The personal glossary primarily serves each student as a ready reference, but you can draw quick reviews from student glossaries and solicit whiteboard answers of, for example, words, definitions, and meaningful sentences based on recent entries.

STEP 5. PLAN MANY OPPORTUNITIES TO APPLY KEY WORDS

For the vocabulary words you've chosen, here are ways to teach them throughout a lesson, organized by the 5 Es model for inquiry-based learning:

> » *Engage* **stage.** Elicit and discuss common definitions and examples from students' prior knowledge. Capture students' informal definitions and examples visually for students who need to see an image and refer to the images throughout the lesson.

> » *Explore* **stage.** Revisit the words students did not know or partially/vaguely defined. Use newly acquired information to refine students' understanding and move from informal to formal, discipline-specific definitions. This is also the phase in which to help students learn the meanings of words that will support their attempts to solve a task, either before they start exploring on their own or as they attempt to express their reasoning in speech or writing.

> » *Explain* **stage.** Toward the end of each lesson, check for students' understanding of the vocabulary and related concepts in order to then reinforce correct definitions and make

notes about important words and concepts that should be revisited in a later lesson. This can also occur while students work in small groups and you roam among them.

» *Elaborate* **stage.** Give students the opportunity to express in more sophisticated ways the academic vocabulary they've learned as they deepen their understanding of concepts by digging deeper into the details or expanding ideas learned in one context to apply them in other contexts and make generalizations.

FIGURE 4.6. Example of Highest-Priority Words

Consider the following sentence from a history textbook.

King George intended to transform the east coast into *colonies*, or lands that were controlled by Britain.

The term *colonies* is the brick (the main discipline concept being introduced). English learners might not know one or more of the function words *intended, transform … in to,* or *or.* In this context, *or* is a mortar word (one that connects concepts) that means "in other words." It introduces a definition of the new concept, rather than introducing a contrast. English learners and students with learning difficulties may likely be confused if a teacher has not explicitly taught this meaning of *or* the first time it was encountered in text.

Students need many opportunities in class discussions and when working with passages of text to hear, repeat, and apply key terms in order to deepen and sustain their understanding of them. Be sure to consciously reuse the key words, emphasizing them when you talk by pausing and perhaps saying the word slightly louder or pointing to the word on a list of key terms posted on a classroom wall.[23]

Tools for Understanding Vocabulary and Concepts

There are many options for teaching vocabulary and helping students organize and understand concepts. The charts at the end of this chapter describe a set of tools and strategies that we hope teachers will find particularly useful for working with English learners and students with learning difficulties. However, although these tools have widely accepted applications for helping students learn words and definitions, they often connote a linear connection among concepts and therefore may not adequately illustrate the interrelated concepts represented by the words. Teachers need to carefully consider their content goals for students when they select tools to support academic vocabulary development. For example, a Word Wall including definitions and illustrations for various types of quadrilaterals may be used throughout a unit to support students in identifying different quadrilaterals. However, during a lesson with the specific goal of helping students compare and contrast characteristics of different quadrilaterals, the teacher might have students use a Features Matrix to identify the characteristics of each type of quadrilateral. The tools presented in this chapter may be particularly useful for such content as logical arguments, identifying evidence, or organizing characteristics of concepts. They may not be helpful for all words or concepts in a discipline. (See chapter 5 for tools that are helpful for representing more complex relationships and for scaffolding concepts.)

Teachers may well combine several of these tools to support students in a given lesson. Regardless of the lesson, the combination of tools would almost surely include Word Walls and glossaries and Sentence

Frames. A Vocabulary Self-Rating can be useful as both a pre- and a post-assessment, alerting students to vocabulary in the upcoming lesson and informing the teacher about vocabulary that may take more or less time to teach and vocabulary that needs reteaching. The Concept Organizer is another tool that can be used daily for perhaps two or three crucial words. List-Group-Label is a way for students to review, allowing them to consolidate conceptual as well as vocabulary knowledge. The Features Matrix is useful both during a lesson and for review.

We recommend that teachers use these tools to support hands-on problem solving, direct instruction, small-group work, and whole-group discussion. To determine which vocabulary building tools to provide for students in a particular lesson, a teacher can try out a couple of them and evaluate how well each works for clarifying particular types of instruction.

WORD WALLS AND GLOSSARIES

Purpose   Word Walls and glossaries help English learners develop and use academic language. Students have important vocabulary words with brief definitions readily available to use when they talk and write about their ideas.

Description   Word Walls (sometimes called Word Charts) list important academic words and phrases along with defining statements (e.g., pictures, informal definitions, example sentences). Words are entered into the Word Wall as they are introduced and may later be organized by topic. These lists are posted around the classroom so that students can easily see and use them. The Word Wall is co-constructed by the teacher and the students to create a public base of knowledge that supports the use of appropriate academic language by all students.

Glossaries are personal collections of important words defined by students and may also include illustrations or other representations. Students may also translate the words into their native languages. In addition to glossary words that students choose for themselves, the teacher may request that all students make specific entries.

An E-word Wall is an alternative to posting charts around the classroom. PowerPoint can be used to create word lists with defining statements, pictures, and sound.[24]

Use   Word Walls can be used at any grade level — high school students, for example, will use more academic vocabulary in their speaking and writing when they have a rich bank of words easily available.[25]

The teacher or a student adds words to wall charts as new words are introduced. In addition to key terms in the course's content area, the Word Wall may include other words — transition words and modifiers — that are important for English learners and students with language difficulties. Students can refer to the charts and apply the words in speaking and writing.

Words might be organized alphabetically or by word families, within topic areas. Word lists can be maintained on a computer for updating and for alternative organizations. Alternatively, large file cards can be tacked to a corkboard with the words on one side and definitions and illustrations on the other side. This allows for categorizing ideas so students see the connection between concepts and can also be used for quick review or assessment.

There is a range of uses for a Word Wall, from simply listing the words on chart paper with a brief visual cue (e.g., sketches, examples) to having a preformatted wall chart to identify word use and add definitions (mirroring what students have in their notebooks). Word Walls can be visible as the teacher is introducing concepts and when students are engaging in problem solving; in this way, it becomes an ongoing tool to model spelling, correct usage, definitions, and so on. The complexity of the format depends on the grade level and the emphasis needed for development of content knowledge.

Parallel to the Word Wall for the class, students might build personal glossaries in their notebooks as a quick reference — especially for writing tasks — including cognates and synonyms in their native languages.

Example   Word Walls and personal glossaries take various forms, depending on their particular purpose. Here is just one example. Teachers will find many additional ways to organize and utilize these tools.

Lists of related words are categorized and their meanings clarified with examples or illustrations. An arrow can be drawn from a definition to the proper location in the illustration.

Graphing		
Predict (v.)	To tell in advance based on experience or reason	
Graph (v. or n.)	A picture of pairs of things (objects)	
Axis (n.)	A (reference) line on a graph	
Vertical (adj.)	Up-and-down	
Horizontal (adj.)	Left-to-right	
Ordered pair (n.)	Location of a point on a graph	
Equation (n.)	A statement that two things (quantities) are equal	

SENTENCE FRAMES

Purpose This tool provides a starting place for saying and writing ideas, as well as a structure that models correct grammar usage and paragraph construction. The support provided by this tool is particularly useful to English learners and students with language difficulties.

Description Students are prompted to create sentences based on frames that provide some sentence parts and leave blanks for others. In some cases, pictures scaffold students' understanding and ability to complete the blank portions of the sentences. Sentence Starters are types of Sentence Frames in which only the start of the sentence is given.

Use Frames help English learners and students with language difficulties produce a complete sentence or paragraph to communicate knowledge. In addition, Sentence Frames can be used to model English grammar, and paragraph frames can be used to model writing skills. Most of a sentence is provided for English learners at early stages (Starting, Emerging), and Sentence Starters are provided for more advanced English learners (Developing, Expanding). Sample Sentence Frames are displayed on the wall for quick reference.

Examples » Sentence Starters: A bank of Sentence Starters is posted in the classroom (e.g., "I agree with _____"; "I don't understand why _____"). The teacher directs students to relevant frames and encourages students to use them during a discussion or writing activity.[26] (See Figure 4.4 for more examples of Sentence Starters.)

» Sentence Frames

Which tide pool animal is your favorite? Why?

My favorite tide pool animal is the _____ because it _____.

How does it protect itself?   It has _____ that it uses to protect itself.

What does it like to eat?   It eats _____. This is its prey.

What likes to eat it?   _____ likes to eat it. This is its predator.

VOCABULARY SELF-RATING

Purpose   This activity alerts students to the key words they will learn and helps them plan and monitor their learning. It helps students be aware of what they know and take responsibility for what they need to learn. The teacher adjusts lessons based on a quick review of students' personal rating sheets.

Description   Students rate their knowledge of key vocabulary words for a lesson. A student's self-rating is personal; it may be shared with the teacher, but it is not graded. Students rate whether they know the word (K), do not know the word (DK), or are not sure (?) at three different points: before the lesson begins, after specific vocabulary instruction, and after instruction on content (at the end of the entire lesson).

Use   » **Introduce phase:** The teacher pronounces each word and students rate their knowledge level. This alerts students to words they need to learn. A quick survey of completed columns alerts the teacher to which words to emphasize.

» **Investigate phase:** Students rate the words again after vocabulary instruction. Students see their growth, and the teacher sees which words need more attention during the content lesson.

» **Summarize phase:** Students rate the words once again and see their growth, and the teacher sees which concepts need further discussion and which content related to the words may not be sufficiently understood.

Example   Students rate their knowledge of key words that are important in the day's lesson.

Vocabulary Self-Rating[27]			
Name:			
Lesson Topic:			Period:
K: I am sure I know it	**DK:** I am sure I don't know it		**?:** I'm not sure
Word (part of speech)	Before Lesson	After Vocabulary Discussion	After Lesson
Organ (n.)			
Amylase (n.)			
Enzyme (n.)			
Absorb (v.)			

CONCEPT ORGANIZER

Purpose	This tool provides one structure for in-depth investigation of the meanings of selected academic vocabulary, which can be particularly helpful for English learners and students with language difficulties.
Description	One Concept Organizer is used for each new word. This tool organizes a variety of ways to understand a word's meaning: using it in sentences, providing synonyms and antonyms, providing a definition, describing characteristics (using phrases that may give slightly different aspects of the word's meaning), and providing examples and nonexamples. If present, a prefix is noted as a clue to a word's meaning.
Use	The teacher gives the word in context, perhaps in a sentence from a class activity. The class brainstorms synonyms, definitions, characteristics, examples, and nonexamples. To complete the Concept Organizer, each student writes his or her own sentence that uses the word. Use the following sequence of steps to teach each new word:

» Point to the word and pronounce it; ask students to repeat the word.

» With class participation, define and describe the word, using at least a synonym or definition and a sentence or brief explanation. Following are some options:

— Identify one or several synonyms or related ideas that students already know.

— List facts/characteristics, perhaps words combined with pictures.

— List examples and nonexamples, using words, sketches, and diagrams.

— Create a student-friendly definition or adapted definition from the course text or a dictionary, or brainstorm a definition with students; write it for everyone to see while students write it on their own organizers.

— Create a sentence that implicitly defines and applies the word or create a brief explanation (from a phrase up to a few sentences).

» Students' Concept Organizers can be written on 5×7 index cards, hole-punched in the top left corner, and organized on a large key ring.

Example	Concept Organizers take various forms, depending on their particular purpose. Here, the Frayer Model is used to organize information related to the mathematical concept of inequality.[28] Many websites present examples in the context of language arts and science or offer more complex or purposive organizers.[29]

Definition	**Facts/Characteristics**
An inequality is a mathematical statement that describes the relationship between two unequal quantities using the symbols $<$, $>$.	Relates two unequal expressions. The value of one expression is greater than or less than the other.

Inequality

Examples	**Nonexamples**
20 oz. $<$ 25 oz.	5 is equal to 4 + 1
p is greater than 3	$a = 197$
$2 \geq x$	$3x$

LIST-GROUP-LABEL

Purpose   This is a tool for organizing words into word families and concept categories to promote schema formation and conceptual understanding. Organizing words in this manner helps make the words easier for students to reference and review and enables students to quickly search within a family of words and recognize relationships among them.

Description   Known words relevant to a lesson are organized by categories given by the teacher or created by student groups. The teacher guides students to see how words are associated. Word families can be classified by relationship (e.g., synonym/antonym) or conceptual characteristics.

Use   The whole class may brainstorm an initial list of words about a topic with the teacher recording the words on the board or a transparency; then small groups organize them by categories and label the categories. When words have multiple meanings in different disciplines, teachers of different subjects can collaborate and teach the multiple meanings explicitly so students see both the connections and subtle differences in meanings.

Examples   In the math example, the right column is blank for students to fill in; the science example shows all entries already filled in.

Numbers	
Types	Characteristics
Whole	
Rational	
Irrational	

Waves	
Types	Characteristics
Mechanical	Gas, liquid, solid
Transverse	Crests, troughs
Longitudinal	Compressions, refractions

FEATURES MATRIX

Purpose A Features Matrix is a visual organizer that can help students see relationships among concept words. It can help clarify similar, but frequently confused terms and can graphically represent similarities and differences within a category.

Description A Features Matrix is a table in which characteristics of a general concept are compared across a range of specific objects or topics that are examples of that general concept. Cells in the matrix usually are marked Yes (present), No (not present), or Maybe (sometimes present).

Use Students work in pairs or small groups to complete a matrix first modeled by the teacher. The matrix may be completed as part of note taking during reading and instruction or to summarize and review afterward. Student groups may be encouraged to add characteristics in a few additional columns on the right. After completing the matrix, students use sentences orally or in writing to describe the characteristics present or not present in an object or topic (e.g., "A square has four sides of equal length and four right angles").

Example This Features Matrix helps students distinguish among various quadrilaterals. Especially helpful for students with learning difficulties, the objects are ordered by the organization or pattern of features.

Type of Quadrilateral	Right Angle	Parallel Sides	Opposite Sides Equal Length
Parallelogram	Maybe	Yes (2 pairs)	Yes
Rhombus	Maybe	Yes (2 pairs)	Yes
Rectangle	Yes	Yes (2 pairs)	Yes
Square	Yes	Yes (2 pairs)	Yes (all four sides)
Trapezoid	No	Yes (1 pair)	Maybe

ENDNOTES FOR CHAPTER 4

[1] Harley, R. (2005). Contented learning. *Language, 4*(9), 22–27; Bay-Williams, J. M., & Herrera, S. (2007). Is "just good teaching" enough to support the learning of English language learners? Insights from sociocultural learning theory. In W. G. Martin, M. E. Strutchens, & P. C. Elliott (Eds.), *The learning of mathematics: Sixty-ninth yearbook* (pp. 43–63). Reston, VA: National Council of Teachers of Mathematics; Freeman, D. J. (2004). Teaching in the context of English-language learners: What we need to know. In M. Sadowski (Ed.), *Teaching immigrant and second-language students: Strategies for success* (pp. 7–20). Cambridge, MA: Harvard Education Press.

[2] Gibbons, P. (2002). *Scaffolding language, scaffolding learning: Teaching second language learners in the mainstream classroom.* Portsmouth, NH: Heinemann.

[3] Short, D. (1993). Assessing integrating language and content. *TESOL Quarterly, 27*(4), 627–656; Bay-Williams, J. M., & Herrera, S. (2007).

[4] Clegg, J. (Ed.). (1996). *Mainstreaming ESL: Case studies in integrating ESL students into the mainstream curriculum.* Clevedon, UK: Multilingual Matters.

[5] Kang, H., & Pham, K. T. (1995, March). *From 1 to Z: Integrating math and language learning* (ERIC Document Reproduction Service No. ED 381 031). Paper presented at the 29th annual meeting of Teachers of English to Speakers of Other Languages, Long Beach, CA.

[6] Martin, T. S. (Ed.). (2007). *Mathematics teaching today* (2nd ed.). Reston, VA: National Council of Teachers of Mathematics.

[7] Anstrom, K. (1999). *Preparing secondary education teachers to work with English language learners: Mathematics* (NCBE Resource Collection Series, No. 14). Washington, DC: National Clearinghouse for Bilingual Education; Cambell, A. E., Adams, V. M., & Davis, G. E. (2007). Cognitive demands and second-language learners: A framework for analyzing mathematics instructional contexts. *Mathematical Thinking and Learning, 9*(1), 3–30; Ellerton, N. F., & Clarkson, P. C. (1996). Language factors in mathematics teaching and learning. In A. J. Bishop, K. Clements, C. Keitel, J. Kilpatrick, & C. Laborde (Eds.), *International handbook of mathematics education* (pp. 987–1033). Dordrecht, Netherlands: Kluwer; Mestre, J. (1988). The role of language comprehension in mathematics and problem solving. In R. Cocking & J. Mestre (Eds.), *Linguistic and cultural influences on learning mathematics* (pp. 201–220). Hillsdale, NJ: Lawrence Erlbaum.

[8] Monroe, E. E., & Panchyshyn, R. (1995). Vocabulary considerations for teaching mathematics. *Childhood Education, 72*(2), 80–83; Laborde, C. (1990). Language and mathematics. In P. Nesher & J. Kilpatrick (Eds.), *Mathematics and cognition: A research synthesis by the International Group for the Psychology of Mathematics Education* (pp. 53–69). Cambridge: Cambridge University Press.

[9] Hayden, D., & Cuevas, G. (1990). *Pre-algebra lexicon.* Washington, DC: Center for Applied Linguistics.

[10] Anstrom, K. (1999).

[11] Jarrett, D. (1999a). *The inclusive classroom: Teaching mathematics and science for students with learning disabilities. It's just good teaching.* Portland, OR: Northwest Regional Educational Laboratory; Jarrett, D. (1999b). *The inclusive classroom: Teaching mathematics and science to English-language learners. It's just good teaching.* Portland, OR: Northwest Regional Educational Laboratory.

[12] Swales, J. M. (2005). Academically speaking. *Language Magazine, 4*(8), 30–34. Conclusions based on analysis of 1.7 million transcribed words of University of Michigan speeches from lectures, office hours, meetings, dissertation defenses, and so forth, collected between 1997 and 2002.

[13] Marzano, R. J., & Pickering, D. J. (2005). *Building academic vocabulary: Teacher's manual.* Alexandria, VA: Association for Supervision and Curriculum Development. The authors have identified nearly 8,000 words in national standards documents in 11 subject areas for grade spans K-2, 3-5, 6-8, and 9-12. The math word list is on pages W1-8.

[14] Dornan, R., Rosen, L. M., & Wilson, M. (2005). Lesson designs for reading comprehension and vocabulary development. In P. A. Richard-Amato & M. A. Snow (Eds.), *Academic success for English language learners* (pp. 248–274). White Plains, NY: Pearson Education.

[15] Stahl, S. A., & Fairbanks, M. M. (1986). The effects of vocabulary instruction: A model-based meta-analysis. *Review of Educational Research, 56*(1), 72–110.

[16] Beck, I. L., McKeown, M. G., & Kucan, L. (2002). *Bringing words to life: Robust vocabulary instruction.* New York: Guilford Press.

[17] Common Core State Standards Initiative. (2010). *English language arts standards.* Retrieved from http://www.corestandards.org/the-standards/english-language-arts-standards

[18] Dutro, S., & Moran, C. (2003). Rethinking English language instruction: An architectural approach. In G. G. Garcia (Ed.), *English learners: Reaching the highest level of English literacy* (pp. 227–258). Newark, DE: International Reading Association.

[19] Lehr, F., Osborn, J., & Hiebert, E. H. (2005). *A focus on vocabulary* [second in the Research-Based Practices in Early Reading Series]. Honolulu, HI: Regional Educational Laboratory at Pacific Resources for Education and Learning. Retrieved from http://www.prel.org/products/re_/ES0419.htm

[20] English and Spanish have many cognates from Latin-based words (e.g., problem/problema, dictionary/diccionario). False cognates, or *amigos falsos*, on the other hand, can trip up students (see http://spanish.about.com/cs/vocabulary/a/obviouswrong.htm for tricky examples such as actual/actual, discutir/discuss, ignorar/ignore, realizar/realize).

[21] Marzano, R. J., & Pickering, D. J. (2005).

[22] Print dictionaries recommended by Kate Kinsella for use with English learners include the following:
The second ELP level (Emerging) in grades 4–9: *The Basic Newbury House Dictionary of American English.* (1998). Florence, KY: Heinle & Heinle.
The third ELP level (Developing) in grades 6–12: *Newbury House Dictionary with Thesaurus.* (2004). Florence, KY: Heinle & Heinle; *Longman Dictionary of American English.* (1997). White Plains, NY: Longman.
The highest ELP level (Bridging) in grades 7–12 and college: *Longman Advanced American Dictionary.* (2000). White Plains, NY: Longman.
Starting through Bridging levels: *Thorndike Barnhart Dictionary.* (1999). Glenview, IL: Scott Forsman.
Wikipedia is becoming a highly popular and easy-to-search online dictionary and encyclopedia, but teachers need to be careful to check that its content is accurate.

[23] Marzano and Pickering offer a range of activities and academically oriented games for reviewing and applying word meanings. See Marzano, R. J., & Pickering, D. J. (2005).

[24] Narkon, D. E., Wells, J. C., & Segal, L. S. (2011, March/April). E-word wall: An interactive vocabulary instruction tool for students with learning disabilities and autism spectrum disorders. *Teaching Exceptional Children, 43*(4), 38–47.

[25] Gibbons, P. (2002).

[26] For Sentence Starters that are appropriate for mathematics through middle school, see Barnett-Clarke, C., & Ramirez, A. (2005). *Discussion builders poster, 4–8.* San Francisco, CA: WestEd. Available from http://www.wested.org/cs/we/view/rs/781

[27] Adapted with author's permission from Kinsella, K. (2007). *Language strategies for active classroom participation.* San Francisco: San Francisco State University. Retrieved as a document named LanguageClassDiscussion.doc from http://www.sccoe.org/depts/ell/kinsella.asp

[28] Frayer, D., Frederick, W. C., & Klausmeier, H. J. (1969). *A schema for testing the level of cognitive mastery.* Madison: Wisconsin Center for Education Research. A brief description is available at http://www.justreadnow.com/strategies/frayer.htm

[29] A variety of graphic organizers for vocabulary development can be downloaded as PDF files, free for classroom use by teachers, from http://www.educationoasis.com/curriculum/GO/vocab_dev.htm

CHAPTER 5

Six Strategies for Scaffolding Content Learning

> **Now that we understand more about how the human brain functions, we know that rather than remediate, we must work to make matches happen between the content to be learned and the learning styles of our students. When the right matches are found, the message we send to struggling students is, 'You can be a successful student!'**
>
> — Susan Winebrenner

The elegant metaphor of *scaffolding* comes to the field of learning from the rough-and-tumble world of construction sites, where temporary frameworks of platforms erected around a building allow workers to reach with their drills, hammers, and brushes areas that otherwise would be out of range.[1] Likewise, a teacher uses scaffolding strategies to temporarily support students while they build new skills and knowledge — at a higher level than they could reach without such assistance.[2] The teacher uses many of the scaffolding strategies when students are working in pairs and trios in the classroom.

It is important to note that scaffolding is not just another word for "helping." As Pauline Gibbons points out, scaffolding "is a special kind of help that assists learners to move toward new skills, concepts, or levels of understanding. Scaffolding is thus a temporary assistance by which a teacher helps a learner know how to do something, so that the learner will later be able to complete a similar task alone."[3] Gibbons warns that scaffolding is not about simplifying a learning task and ultimately watering down curriculum. The importance of scaffolding is that it allows a teacher to provide authentic and challenging tasks to all students, with the supports that allow each student to be successful. The teacher's goal is to move learners from dependence on teacher-designated strategies to independent application of strategies for their own purposes and in a variety of settings. When students have sufficiently internalized the strategy and understand its purpose, process, and various uses, they apply it independently during group and individual learning tasks. When students have internalized a strategy, a teacher-initiated scaffold can be withdrawn or replaced by a scaffold that is different in type, purpose, or intensity.

For example, a teacher might present a specific graphic organizer and fill it in with student input, then fade out the intensity of guidance over a series of lessons. The class reaches a point at which students just need a cue about the lesson topic or objective, the teacher checks that all students selected the appropriate graphic organizer, and students fill it in individually or in small groups. The appropriate graphic organizer might be a story map for a fiction text in language arts or a bubble map in science, and the cue for science might begin with a content objective, such as "You will identify the properties of five minerals in the tray at your group's table using an appropriate graphic organizer."

All students benefit from teachers who guide and support them as they construct new knowledge. English learners and students with learning difficulties require scaffolds tailored to fit their learning needs if they are to master a rigorous, standards-aligned curriculum. Every student has the right to equal access to the same challenging curriculum appropriate for that grade level. Scaffolding is a way for teachers to keep content at a high level yet still provide access to the diverse learners in the classroom. Tailoring support for a student with ADHD, for example, could involve as little as 10 minutes of direct instruction followed by 2 minutes of student responses and checking for understanding or assigning 5 to 10 rather than 20 repetitive mathematics problems as homework. For an English learner, it might mean assigning a strategic subset of 20 vocabulary words for homework and assessment.

The scaffolding strategies in this chapter benefit all students in the classroom and can be applied to the whole class but may need to be tailored to fit different types of learners or individual students. Tailoring, or further differentiating a strategy, means that the teacher modifies the use of a strategy to give somewhat different kinds of support to students at different English language development levels or students with different ways of learning to ensure that all students have equal access to rigorous content.

SIX EFFECTIVE, PRACTICAL STRATEGIES FOR SCAFFOLDING LEARNING

We assume that many teachers have some level of familiarity with most or all of the strategies we describe here. If a strategy is entirely new for a teacher, though, we encourage using other resource materials or experienced colleagues to learn more about its purpose and implementation. However, we purposefully selected strategies that are fairly quick and easy to learn. These are strategies that can be applied to teaching in any content area, can be integrated and embedded into doable differentiated lessons, and can be used frequently (even daily) in the classroom. Also, research and professional literature has identified these strategies as being effective with the general student population, English learners, and students with learning difficulties.[4,5,6] (See Appendix A for a chart of the research and professional literature supporting the strategies recommended in this guidebook.)

Based on these criteria, the six strategies we recommend for scaffolding content are:

1. Visuals	4. Cues
2. Think-Pair-Share	5. Think Aloud
3. KWL+	6. Summarization

We provide brief descriptions of each of these strategies here, and the tools and strategies guides at the end of this chapter provide more detailed descriptions and examples for each strategy in a format that can be used for easy reference.

Visuals

This strategy consists of using nonlinguistic representations (such as photos, models, real objects) and spatial-linguistic representations (such as graphic organizers that contain terms or very brief text in a spatial organization) to visually represent ideas and relationships among ideas. Visuals are concrete representations that can be an important and effective addition to direct instruction — a teacher can scaffold his or her talking with visuals such as objects, videos, gestures, items, or terms on a chart or board that the teacher points to and, most important, graphic organizers. Physically modeling or demonstrating can also be classified as using visuals.

HOW TONY LEARNS BEST

In a moment of introspection in 10th grade, Tony (an English learner with autism spectrum disorder and auditory processing difficulty) said, "I learn best when I can see it and hear it at the same time. Then I can repeat it as many times as I want. I pick up new information each time I see it." In the classroom, Tony can repeat a brief lesson by watching a video, and the teacher can introduce vocabulary and concepts briefly for the whole class and then follow up by having students work on small-group tasks that repeat the key vocabulary and concepts in a variety of ways.

Think-Pair-Share

To use Think-Pair-Share, the teacher poses a challenging, open-ended question and gives students a brief time to think (usually from five seconds to one minute). Student pairs then discuss their ideas for one or more minutes. And lastly, pairs share ideas with a larger group or the whole class. (See the section on student-led instruction in chapter 1 for ideas for forming pairs and small groups.) Think-Write-Pair-Share is an adaptation in which students jot down their ideas before discussing with a partner; the writing step holds each student more accountable and the teacher can read responses while pairs are sharing, but it may need to be adapted for students who struggle just to compose a brief idea (e.g., students may be given the choice to write, illustrate, or record an idea). A graphic organizer can be used to help support this strategy, using four columns: "Question," "What I thought," "What my partner thought," and "What we will share." The Pair-Share steps can come after thinking, reading, or writing; in common are time for individuals to reflect or think critically followed by time for pairs/groups to rehearse and rephrase ideas and to practice social skills, such as active listening and disagreeing respectfully.

Think-Pair-Share is quick, encourages all students to participate, and encourages students to perform as experts (not just the teacher) by shifting some control for the learning process from the teacher to the student groups. Often the teacher will need to model the expected behaviors of group work (what students say and do) until students have internalized the rules of social learning. Collaborative grouping provides opportunities to teach social skills, academic discourse, and civics.

KWL+

This strategy consists of publicly recording students' responses to questions about what they already know (K) and what they want (W) to know as they begin a new lesson, and then at the end of the lesson recording what students have learned (L). The "+" aspect of KWL+ refers to the final step of making connections among the three categories of information. KWL+ is a special type of graphic organizer.

Cues

Cues are advance organizers, hints, and prompting questions by the teacher.[7] *Advance organizers* orient students to upcoming important content. *Hints* directly frame or preview the learning. *Questions* reinforce what has been taught and check for understanding.

The teacher uses cues, such as reflecting on a prior lesson or presenting an advance organizer at the beginning of a day's lesson, to help students recall and start connecting to prior knowledge. During the lesson, and as part of checking for understanding, the teacher uses prompts to elicit more information or expand on an idea. The teacher guides student thinking with cues as questions or statements, particularly as an advance organizer during the *engage* stage of the lesson and when checking for understanding.

Think Aloud

Using Think Aloud, the teacher verbalizes his or her own thought processes or models academic discourse, such as modeling how students should interact during group work. Think Aloud needs to be supported with visuals (e.g., pointing to parts of a graphic organizer displayed on the wall, indicating specific words or passages in the text) as the teacher gives students insight into what he or she is thinking while reading text. Before students start a small-group task, the teacher might need to model a thinking strategy, indicating appropriate ways to interact during small-group discussions. For Think Aloud to be effective, the teacher must make the purpose explicit and give students chances to practice the strategy to internalize it. There is a base of research on Think Aloud showing that it is particularly effective with English learners who also have learning difficulties.[8]

Summarization

This strategy can be as simple as the teacher summarizing important information at the conclusion of direct instruction or group work; but more often, the teacher should have students do the summarizing. When students complete a segment of active learning, for example, the teacher might ask them to summarize important information, which provides an opportunity for the teacher to check for understanding. In summarizing, students must comprehend and distill information into a parsimonious, synthesized form — in their own words. The Summarization tools and strategies guide on page 104 includes an example of a step-by-step process for summarizing a text by deciding what is unimportant and can be deleted, then deciding what important information might be rephrased or kept as is, and finally, producing the summary.

Note taking is a form of summarization and may occur during teacher talk or while a group conducts a science experiment or concludes a discussion about a story, alternative mathematics strategies, or social events or historical persons.[9] For English learners at early language development stages and for some students with learning difficulties and other struggling writers, one way to scaffold note taking is to give students the teacher's notes as Sentence Frames with blanks where the students can write in key ideas. The teacher might differentiate by giving a mostly completed template to some students and a less completed template, which requires more writing, for the more proficient students. (Generally, students should not be given fully completed notes so they maintain an active role in the learning process and can practice summarization.) Completing Sentence Frames or writing with a keyboard (rather than having to write by hand) can support many students with learning difficulties, particularly students with AS, who often have fine motor skill difficulties, and students with ADHD and SLD, who typically have difficulty organizing thoughts, sequencing information, and identifying main idea and details. Also, the teacher may need to chunk talking by stating limited new information and giving students with learning difficulties time to process and summarize it in notes, and then repeat the process for each chunk of information. This is a procedure that benefits all students, especially when introducing a new concept or integrating information.

When the teacher intersperses chunks of information with summarization activities, students can store much more information in long-term memory than when the teacher spends a long time providing information without giving breaks for students to summarize. When students are given time — ideally during small-group discussions and tasks — to reflect, repeat, rephrase, connect, and apply information, these opportunities help English learners and students with learning difficulties to not be overwhelmed with too much oral language, too many concepts, or missing connections. Summarization tasks give students time to process new information and give teachers time to check for understanding of each chunk of information.

In the sections that follow, we describe four important considerations to help teachers implement these key strategies: using strategies that work for *all* students; extending and adapting strategies to support diverse learners; combining or making connections among strategies; and providing a classroom climate that supports these scaffolding strategies.

USING STRATEGIES THAT WORK FOR ALL STUDENTS

Some instructional strategies work well for all or most students and do not need differentiation for students at different English learner levels or with different learning difficulties. When the teacher combines visuals with teacher talk, for example, it benefits all students who are visual/spatial learners, including English learners with limited English vocabulary and students with learning difficulties struggling to process complex ideas presented orally.

Two strategies described above — Visuals and Think-Pair-Share — are what we consider to be the two quintessential strategies because they are effective for all students and can be especially helpful to English learners and students with learning difficulties. We highly recommend that teachers frequently:

1. support direct instruction (or teacher talk) with visuals, and

2. engage students in active learning with Think-Pair-Share.

Using visuals, such as simply pointing to a picture, can help convey the meaning of words for English learners who may not be able to detect and process all of the English the teacher says. The teacher might also add function words or connecting words to the lines connecting concepts in a bubble map to help

English learners who have not yet learned how to use many of the function/connector words that most native English speakers know. Conveying connections among ideas by using a graphic organizer might help a student with ASD to form a mental picture of cause and effect, compare and contrast, or systems/cycles. Students might benefit from being able to refer to visuals such as a Word Wall, Sentence Starters, or a graphic organizer to aid in communicating ideas. English learners at an early language development stage might draw pictures, an illustration, or a storyboard and perhaps complete a graphic organizer instead of being asked to write long responses (e.g., paragraph, essay) as a modified assessment. Using a graphic organizer to write lengthy text and breaking the writing task into parts can help students with learning difficulties. Manipulating objects in mathematics, conducting an experiment in science, and reenacting historical events can be powerful visual, tactile, and kinesthetic learning activities.

In addition to recommending frequent use of visuals, we also recommend that teachers plan to use the majority of each class period for strategic groups of students to practice using academic language and engage in social, inquiry-based learning. As stated in chapter 1, many English learners and students with learning difficulties need repetition and rephrasing of ideas and need comfortable situations to ask questions and volunteer answers. Small-group work, such as in Think-Pair-Share, addresses these needs.

EXTENDING AND ADAPTING STRATEGIES TO SUPPORT DIVERSE LEARNERS

A specific strategy need not be limited to a one-time use within one stage of the lesson. A strategy can be used throughout much of a lesson. For example, the teacher may begin using visuals such as a Word Wall or a graphic organizer during the *engage* stage, then add and expand words and concepts during the *explore* stage, and guide the students to apply their language expression skills during the *explain* and *elaborate* stages. Chapter 7 presents a sample lesson plan outline that shows how strategies are used throughout the 5 Es. And routine use of a strategy throughout the year helps all students focus on learning concepts rather than on learning how to use new strategies.

Any of the six strategies can be adapted for use in different ways at different points in a lesson or during the year. For example, a teacher might first distribute a blank graphic organizer for small-group members to complete by pooling their knowledge and skills. Then, for students to individually use the graphic organizer, the teacher might distribute the template in two or three states of completion, particularly for English learners at early stages of language development and certain students with learning difficulties. If the organizer is used during note taking, the teacher might also give students the alternative of creating a traditional outline (topic, indented subtopics) or writing on a partially completed template.

When the teacher and English learners share the same primary language, the teacher might encourage English learners to use their primary language when they do not know certain words in English for communicating what they know. For example, a visual organizer might contain some text in English and some in Spanish, helping Spanish-speaking students to communicate what they know and helping the teacher identify what they know and what vocabulary they need in order to express themselves in English (and perhaps in Spanish, where bilingualism is valued). As another example, a teacher might group students by primary language, allowing group members to use as much of their primary language as needed to express themselves during the first two parts of Think-Pair-Share, then the teacher might request that they use

English when groups share with the whole class. We have observed an eighth grade science lesson in which a group of Spanish speakers interchangeably used English and Spanish and one student translated English-to-Spanish for a member who was at the Entering level of proficiency as an English learner (understood very little English). The teacher did not speak Spanish, and a lesson objective was to use certain English vocabulary words appropriately, so whole-class sharing was in English.

When planning an advance organizer as a cue, teachers should consider students with ASD who have specific topical interests and try to relate the lesson to those interests. This is personalizing instruction, requiring that teachers get to know their students as individuals. Asking students to complete a personal profile in the first class meeting is one way to discover each student's strengths and weaknesses, learning preferences, and interests and aspirations. In a middle or high school, the personal profile could be completed in the homeroom or first-period class and then shared with other teachers; doing this electronically has many advantages.

Here are brief examples that shift from dependence on the teacher to student self-directed learning. The three examples use the context of a graphic organizer, but fading from intensive teacher support to greater student self-learning, as exemplified here, is applicable to all of the strategies, not just for using graphic organizers.

» The teacher shows a model of a graphic organizer such as a bubble map, explains its purpose, and shows how to use it with one or two very specific examples, starting with a nonacademic topic with low cognitive demand, such as characteristics of students' shoes by gender. The teacher then shows an academic topic with a slightly higher cognitive demand as practice for high cognitive demand tasks.

» Students work in groups to apply the same graphic organizer in a few lessons and then apply it independently. Certain students may still be given partially complete templates according to their need for scaffolding.

» As students learn how to use a bank of graphic organizers, the teacher guides students to select the appropriate organizer for new topics or tasks. When the teacher systematically and frequently has students use the organizers, students build fluency and self-reliance in selecting and completing a graphic organizer.

COMBINING OR MAKING CONNECTIONS AMONG STRATEGIES

Rather than treating each strategy as independent of others, we recommend seeing the strategies as interdependent and trying to integrate two or more strategies for what might be a synergistic effect.[10] Teachers should identify connections among strategies and make those connections explicit for students. For example, cues (e.g., Sentence Frames) and visuals (e.g., diagrams, brief graphic organizers) can be embedded in note taking, one kind of summarizing. As another example, a teacher might think aloud about ways to agree or disagree and refer to placards of Sentence Starters (see chapter 4, Figure 4.4) as a way to model expectations for students before they begin a Think-Pair-Share or other small-group task involving an exchange of peer-to-peer ideas.

Figure 5.1 shows connections among the six scaffolding strategies, and they are superimposed on a rectangle that depicts which strategies are used primarily during teacher-led instruction versus during student-led learning.

Notice the lines and arrows connecting the strategies in Figure 5.1. A line represents an associative connection, and an arrow represents a direction of influence in which strategy A has a causal impact on strategy B or simply helps students to respond appropriately during strategy B. Notice that there are connections between all six strategies. As previously mentioned, these particular strategies were selected in part because they can and should be integrated during a lesson.

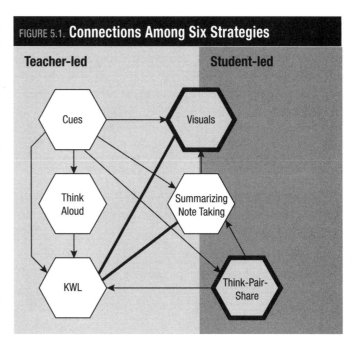

FIGURE 5.1. **Connections Among Six Strategies**

Cues are related to Think Aloud and visuals. For example, a teacher might provide hints or models as the teacher thinks aloud and uses visuals to support that talking — pointing to pictures and words in the margins of the science book as the teacher makes sense of the main content or locates an answer to a question at the end of a unit. The arrow from Cues to KWL+ represents the use of an advance organizer and prompting questions to elicit responses for the "K" and the "W" as well as questions and perhaps hints (including planned Sentence Starters) during the "L" phase. During teacher talk, the teacher provides Cues about what is especially important to summarize as students take notes. The arrow from Cues to Think-Pair-Share represents when the teacher uses hints and questions to guide student thinking during small-group work or whole-class sharing of ideas. Regarding small-group work, the teacher provides cues when facilitating a target group or monitoring all groups and briefly intervening in a group that needs guidance.

A teacher might use Think Aloud as a hint or model when students are unable to offer ideas during KWL+, Think-Pair-Share, or summarizing. For example, in a lesson on erosion during the "K" of KWL+, a teacher might say, "I'm thinking of seeing what rain does to the earth where I live. I remember watching rain fall from the roof of my house and seeing little grooves and puddles of water where it hit the dirt."

KWL+ is a visual, a graphic organizer with three columns to summarize ideas. Think-Pair-Share can involve all students in generating ideas to add to the KWL+ chart instead of requiring students to think and volunteer answers individually.

When summarizing connected concepts, students — particularly English learners, students with learning difficulties, and other students who struggle with handwriting and/or composing a text — might use visuals such as pictures and graphic organizers, or voice recordings instead of writing sentences, paragraphs, or essays, when that level of writing skill is far above their level of language development or when they struggle with the mechanics of handwriting.

Think-Pair-Share is a scaffold for students who have yet to master the skill of summarizing ideas. It is appropriate during instruction but not during summative and some formative assessments when the teacher wants to know what each student has learned and wants to measure an individual's progress over time to determine if classroom instructional strategies are working.

PROVIDING A CLASSROOM CLIMATE THAT SUPPORTS THESE SCAFFOLDING STRATEGIES

These scaffolding strategies should be intertwined throughout a lesson as the teacher moves through the 5 Es teaching framework (introduced in chapter 1) of *engage, explore, explain, elaborate,* and *evaluate.* In such a classroom, each student is not learning from the teacher in isolation of other students. In the inclusive, differentiated classroom, each student is a member of a small team, often a pair or a triad, discussing ideas, reading, writing, solving problems, and investigating phenomena. Each student also is part of the whole class and interacts individually and through team responses with the teacher during direct instruction. When a student orally answers a teacher's question during whole-class instruction, representing his or her own idea or a team's idea, all other students have the opportunity to respond (e.g., agree, disagree). In small teams, students should learn from each other. They may rephrase what the teacher said, perhaps saying it in a way that other team members can better understand. This includes using their primary language. Each student should feel valued and responsible to be there every day because teammates depend on the student. Diverse learners thrive in such a social learning environment supported by scaffolding strategies.

The teacher should establish a classroom climate that lowers anxiety of English learners and students with learning difficulties so that they can participate and know that other students will not ridicule them. It helps to discuss classroom rules that underpin using the scaffolding strategies, such as respecting others' opinions, valuing diversity of beliefs, and other acceptable social learning behaviors. Having laid down the ground rules, the teacher should then guide students as they begin to practice social learning.

Classroom rules should be stated positively, identifying the expected behavior (e.g., "Use your soft voice during group talk" instead of "Don't shout"). Ideally, the teacher should guide students to co-develop the classroom rules as a first step in student ownership of their learning process. It is important to keep in mind that students who are highly engaged and feeling successful are less likely to misbehave; misbehaving and tuning out are often the result of boredom or frustration. In *Discipline with Dignity*, the authors encourage differentiating and personalizing instruction as key ways to establish and maintain a positive, safe, respectful classroom climate.[11] Those key ways can be distilled into two suggestions:

» Teachers should differentiate instruction based on students' strengths and should vary their style of presentation (between direct instruction and small-group discussions); and

» Teachers should listen to what students are thinking and feeling and should ask them what they need from the teacher.

HOW TO SCAFFOLD READING MATERIALS

One way teachers can differentiate instruction that is particularly helpful for English learners and students with language difficulties is to make adaptations to the reading materials used for the class. English learners at low English language proficiency levels and students with learning difficulties, as well as other students struggling with literacy skills, may have difficulty with independently reading texts, particularly academic texts. But if the texts are modified, these struggling students will not be so dependent on scaffolding strategies during instruction or group work involving reading.

In general, we recommend that students do not read long text passages until they are well into the *explore* or *explain* stage of a lesson, after the teacher has explained key unknown words, terms, and phrases (which can be helpful for English learners) and certain function words or conceptual connections (which can be helpful for students with learning difficulties). We also recommend that students who struggle with literacy skills not always be required to read the district-adopted text — there should be options such as alternative texts at different readability levels as long as the core content is the same as in the grade-level texts. We offer four options below, each of which describes steps for planning instruction using scaffolds with different types of reading materials. We do *not* endorse using just one option all of the time in all content areas — a struggling reader should experience the district-adopted texts as part of the core curriculum, but the student should experience success or accomplishment rather than frustration and failure. We suggest that teachers consider these four options and use professional judgment in choosing what is best for certain students in certain contexts rather than always trying to use the same option.

OPTION 1: USING UNALTERED TEXT

English learners at the Developing and lower English language proficiency levels and students with learning difficulties whose reading levels are more than two grades below grade level may be able to comprehend some short excerpts reading independently but will likely have difficulty with complete texts or book chapters.

Some students with learning difficulties also may need accommodations, such as text in digital format and assistive technology. Examples include: large print, chunking, enhanced spacing between the lines, hyperlinks to vocabulary definitions or video clips to demonstrate concepts, audio format, text-to-speech software, voice recognition software, and text using a different text-background color combination for students who are irritated by black print on white paper.

Whereas struggling readers in the primary grades may need to focus on decoding skills, struggling readers at the secondary school level need to focus on comprehension skills. Reading Apprenticeship and Collaborative Strategic Reading are two instructional models for improving content area literacy and supporting students in comprehending grade-level texts.[12,13]

The following steps will help all struggling readers to access content in a text.

> **Step 1.** Identify excerpts in a conceptual unit of study that address the most critical or essential information that students who struggle with English literacy need to understand.

Step 2. Provide interesting, concrete activities to front-load key content and functional vocabulary in context, building conceptual understanding during the *engage* and *explore* stages. Students can then reference Word Walls and graphic organizers when they read the excerpts.

Step 3. Provide the excerpts along with advance organizers and meaningful questions for students to answer. Use Think Aloud to model reading strategies and note taking so that students learn reading skills to make sense of text and record information.

Step 4. Have students collaboratively read text excerpts in small groups as part of the *explain* or *elaborate* stages using notes taken during the *explore* stage and, if needed, model reading strategies that apply to this task.

OPTION 2: USING ANNOTATED TEXT EXCERPTS

English learners at the Developing level may be able to comprehend annotated excerpts reading independently. English learners at the Starting and Emerging levels and some students with learning difficulties will likely have difficulty independently reading and comprehending annotated text excerpts. The steps below will help these students use annotated excerpts to comprehend written content.

Step 1. Identify excerpts in a conceptual unit that address the most critical or essential information that these students need to understand. Annotate the excerpts by highlighting key words, defining or clarifying key concepts with notes in the margin, and/or adding illustrations. Make copies to hand out to the students if technology is not available for this purpose.

Step 2. Provide concrete activities to front-load key content and functional vocabulary in context, building conceptual understanding during the *engage* and *explore* stages. Students can then reference Word Walls, concept organizers, and graphic organizers throughout the lesson. Introduce the annotated excerpts during the *explore* stage.

Step 3. Provide students with meaningful questions to answer, and use Think Aloud to model reading comprehension strategies so that students will be able to apply their reading skills to make sense of the annotated text and to record information.

Step 4. Have English learners collaboratively read text excerpts in small groups as part of the elaborate stage.

OPTION 3: USING READING MATERIALS AT VARIOUS READABILITY LEVELS

English learners at Emerging and higher levels can independently read and comprehend texts at their readability level. English learners at the Starting level likely cannot independently read and comprehend brief texts at the lowest possible readability level, but can comprehend some ideas with assisted reading and pictures or illustrations depicting the key ideas. Students with reading comprehension difficulties may or may not benefit from reading-leveled texts independently but likely can benefit when student pairs or triads work together on reading and answering questions. When students with different texts form a group, the exchange of common and unique information can benefit all students.

Use of leveled texts is temporary — struggling readers should have interventions to rapidly increase their reading skills, although vocabulary acquisition may take a long time for older English learners. It is crucial that texts at various readability levels address the grade-level standards with the same rigor to ensure that all students have access to the same curriculum. When it is important that all students experience a difficult grade-level text, such as one of Shakespeare's plays, options 1 or 2 should be considered, along with other instructional scaffolds discussed in this chapter.

Step 1. Find texts at students' readability levels that explain key ideas in content standards, with help from the librarian, ELD/English teachers, reading specialists, colleagues, district experts, and Internet sites.

Step 2. Front-load key academic vocabulary and build conceptual understanding during the *engage* and *explore* stages. Introduce contextualized and visually rich text resources during the *explore* and/or *explain* stages.

Step 3. Provide meaningful questions for the students to answer, and model note taking using specific organizers, charts, tables, or graphs appropriate for the task.

Step 4. Each small group may be assigned the same or different text levels. Have students read independently or (better) in pairs and then discuss and, using a poster, annotate concepts independently and/or as a group.

OPTION 4: USING TECHNOLOGY

English learners at the Emerging and higher levels can read texts appropriate to their English proficiency level. They can gain further understanding of a topic through investigations, experiments, group projects, field trips, and multimedia technology, such as audio and video clips. Students with reading comprehension difficulties will benefit from this approach, especially when working in a pair or triad.

Step 1. Depending on need, model the use of new technology. Technology and other interactive media may be introduced as part of the *explore, explain,* or *elaborate* stages to support concept development. Front-load key conceptual ideas and key academic vocabulary in context as described in option 3, with the addition of available interactive media.

Step 2. Provide options for students to access content and represent their understanding. Have students choose multimedia resources according to ability and personal interests. Students may produce portfolios and demonstrate understanding using a variety of media tools.

Step 3. You might assign students to small groups, rotate them through stations that include technology use, or have them work independently. Serve as facilitator and coach, consulting and conferencing with students individually or in small groups about their portfolio work.

These options pertain to written texts and other supportive media. However, this stops short of teaching students content literacy skills — how to read and write in different disciplines. The scaffolding strategies can be used to teach literacy skills in a discipline with the goal of enabling students to read disciplinary texts with understanding and making use of that information to build and apply knowledge. For example, a teacher can use the Think Aloud strategy while pointing to areas of the text projected on a screen to say how he or she actively reads for comprehension. It is beyond the scope of this guidebook to delve deeper into effective strategies for teaching literacy skills to struggling readers, so we encourage interested readers to explore other resource materials and professional development opportunities, such as Reading Apprenticeship® developed by the Strategic Literacy Initiative at WestEd.[14]

ANNOTATING TEXT TO OVERCOME HOMEWORK STRUGGLES

Tony, an English learner with autism spectrum disorder, struggled to understand a geometry homework assignment consisting of a set of items in which a triangle was drawn on an x- and y-axis grid. The direction was to "copy each figure onto graph paper, and then use the given rule to transform the figure. Identify the type of transformation given by each rule." To solve the transformation, an item might give "$R(x,y) = (-x,y)$." The teacher had provided intensive help for Tony during class, but when he confronted his homework later in the evening, he had no idea what to do, saying, "I just don't get math, and I can't remember anything that my teacher said."

A proficient reader would notice the key words *transform* and *rule* and then look back in the textbook to find rules of transformation, but Tony needed help to make those connections. Tony's father decided to look through the book and annotate the text. He found definitions for three types of transformations but no rules, and then found three highlighted activities with procedural steps to transform a triangle. He was able to identify the second step in each method as the major piece of information for creating a rule. The last step in each activity box was "Express your method as a set of rules …" At the end of the activity box for rotations was the expression "$R(x,y) = (?,?)$."

To annotate the textbook so Tony could complete the homework items, his father drew arrows from the expression(s) at the end of each activity box to the second step (or other appropriate step) in the box and labeled them "Rule(s)." He wrote:

Step 1: Copy the triangle on graph paper and write the coordinates (x and y numbers) for each vertex. Repeat this for all of the homework items.

Step 2: Look at the capital letter in the homework item and find that same letter in one of the three activity boxes (e.g., R).

Step 3: Follow the arrow to the step in the activity to see if you are to add or multiple x or y or multiple both x and y.

Step 4: Go back to the homework item. Look at its expression to see what to do to x or y. For example, $(x + 3, y)$ means add 3 to x and leave y unchanged, $(x, -y)$ means multiply y by -1 and leave x unchanged.

Step 5: Do the math function (add or subtract, or multiply) for each vertex of the triangle to draw the new transformed triangle. Look at the activity title to label each of your transformed triangles.

Tony completed the homework items and showed them to his father. Most were correct, but a few were incorrect because Tony confused the x- and y-coordinates in his working memory (a symptom of autism spectrum disorder). His father asked Tony if the steps on the sheet of paper and arrows in the activity boxes (annotated text) helped him. Tony replied, "Step 1 was good because I could concentrate on that one thing and get it out of the way for all the items. Step 2 was a hint for me to find the right rule. Steps 3 to 5 were still tough for me, but I got almost all the items right. Why couldn't the book just show these steps for students like me whose brains just don't understand math?"

PROGRESSING OVER TIME TO GREATER EXPERTISE WITH THESE STRATEGIES

It takes time for a teacher to progress from novice to expert in the use of a new strategy. Four steps to becoming an expert with the strategies presented in this chapter are:[15]

1. Preparing to use one or more strategies — learning more from resource materials or colleagues, as needed.

2. Using some strategies sometimes — working on the basics or mechanics of implementation.

3. Using strategies frequently — becoming more comfortable as students become more successful.

4. Refining and targeting strategies — tailoring strategies to fit different topics and students who learn in different ways and seamlessly flowing from one strategy to another or embedding one strategy in another.

VISUALS

Purpose	Usually, the primary method of presenting new knowledge to students is in linguistic form — by using words — but only a portion of students in the classroom learn best by listening to the teacher. When teachers help students create nonlinguistic representations of new learning, as with illustrations or symbols or by organizing information graphically, it increases students' opportunities to learn. The more those students experience and use multiple systems of representation, linguistic and nonlinguistic, the better they are able to think about and recall knowledge. English learners and some students with learning difficulties need nonlinguistic supports during teacher talk. Visuals lessen the linguistic load and scaffold learning rigorous content for students who struggle with linguistic representations of the content.
Description	Visuals can be real objects, models, demonstrations, pictures, illustrations, and video clips or other visual media (e.g., webcasts, animations). The concept of visuals can be extended to include school field trips and family experiences, such as time spent in other countries and knowledge of other (written) languages and cultures.
	Graphic organizers are visual tools for recording and recalling important information. Organizers may have labels (words, phrases) and illustrations and use spatial orientation with lines or arrows to show organization and associative (lines) or causal/sequential (arrows) connections. Common graphic organizers include: KWL charts, T-charts (two columns to show what is similar or dissimilar for a row of objects/concepts), and the variety of examples that appear in the tools and strategies guides and charts on the following pages.
Use for English learners and students with learning difficulties	Graphic organizers can be used for ELD or content area instruction and assessment. They can be used in conjunction with lecture and discussion; they can be embedded in the use of KWL charts and note taking. They can be useful learning and assessment tools, especially for English learners who are not yet adept at using complex grammar and function words to connect ideas in written English. During learning, graphic organizers support teacher talk and student-student oral discussion, helping English learners see the language that they are unable to aurally comprehend. Seeing concise statements and concept connections helps students with learning difficulties process new information. During assessment, graphic organizers help English learners and students with learning difficulties show and communicate what they understand as an alternative to or in support of long, complex oral or written responses (e.g., many connected sentences). A graphic organizer can help all students organize their thoughts before writing an essay or research report.
	There are many graphic organizers in books and on websites. It can be beneficial for a school or school district to identify a core set of organizers for different uses so that students, after initially learning a certain organizer, can focus their attention on the content to be learned in other classes and higher grade levels. Of course, establishing a core set of organizers also benefits teachers — they can move right to teaching content instead of teaching their personal organizers.
Examples	A science teacher always gives directions orally and in writing for small groups before they begin an investigation. When teaching a class that includes English learners at the Starting and Emerging levels and a student with a learning difficulty who "thinks in pictures," the teacher starts with simply worded step-by-step directions and then creates illustrations (e.g., water pouring from a beaker) to substitute for the words. The teacher combines the words and illustrations as scaffolded directions for all students to see during the group investigation.
	The tools and strategies guides and charts on the following pages show several examples of organizers that can be used to represent information visually. According to Thinking Maps, Inc., there are eight types of graphic organizers corresponding to research about the eight ways people think.[16] A variety of websites and other resources feature graphic organizers, tools for generating graphic organizers, and student samples across a range of content areas.[17]

TYPES OF GRAPHIC ORGANIZERS

CIRCLE MAP FOR DEFINING IN CONTEXT

Outer ring objects are related to the central object. One type of circle map, Frayer's Concept Organizer, has four boxes to explain a word or term; there are a variety of attributes (box labels) that could be selected, based on what best defines a particular word/term. Consistent use of specific object shapes can help students with learning difficulties (see story and character maps[18]).

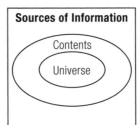

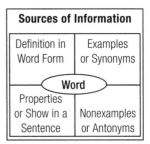

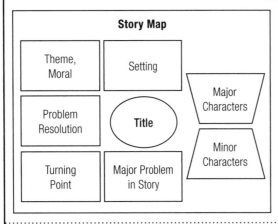

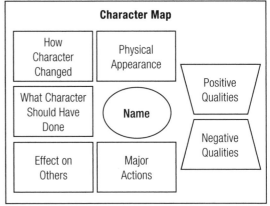

TREE MAP FOR CLASSIFYING AND GROUPING

Tree maps are particularly applicable in science to show hierarchical relationships. The map on the left might also be used in language arts to show synonyms and antonyms for a word in each column.

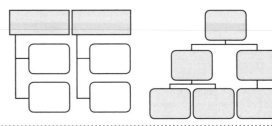

BUBBLE MAP FOR DESCRIBING WITH ADJECTIVES

The target word or term could be a person, place, or thing in any discipline. Bubbles surrounding the target word/term describe it and usually are adjectives but could also be short phrases.

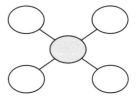

TYPES OF GRAPHIC ORGANIZERS (CONTINUED)

DOUBLE BUBBLE MAP FOR COMPARING AND CONTRASTING

The traditional graphic organizer has been a Venn diagram; however, the shape of two overlapping bubbles does not afford much room for what is similar and dissimilar. The double bubble format allows plenty of space and makes it easy to see each word/term as a separate object and its relationship to one or both target words/terms.

Dissimilar (Unique)   Similar (Common)   Dissimilar (Unique)

FLOW MAP FOR SEQUENCING AND ORDERING

Appropriate for time series or flow of a process.

Exposition ⟩ Rising Action ⟩ Climax ⟩ Falling Action ⟩ Resolution ⟩

MULTIFLOW MAP FOR ANALYZING CAUSES AND EFFECTS

Cause 1
Cause 2
Cause 3

Primary Effect or Problem Conflict

which then …

Effect 1
Effect 2

BRACE MAP FOR IDENTIFYING PART/WHOLE RELATIONSHIPS

Body Systems
  Digestive — • Mouth •
  Circulatory — • Heart •
  Respiratory — • Nose •
  Nervous — • Brain •

BRIDGE MAP FOR SEEING ANALOGIES

Natthaphon is

$\dfrac{\text{son}}{\text{dad}}$ ∧ $\dfrac{\text{nephew}}{\text{uncle}}$ ∧ $\dfrac{\text{grandson}}{\text{grandma}}$

Metric System … equals …

$\dfrac{\text{100 mm}}{\text{1 cm}}$ ∧ $\dfrac{\text{100 cm}}{\text{1 m}}$ ∧ $\dfrac{\text{1000 m}}{\text{1 km}}$

GRAPHIC ORGANIZER AS NOTE TAKING

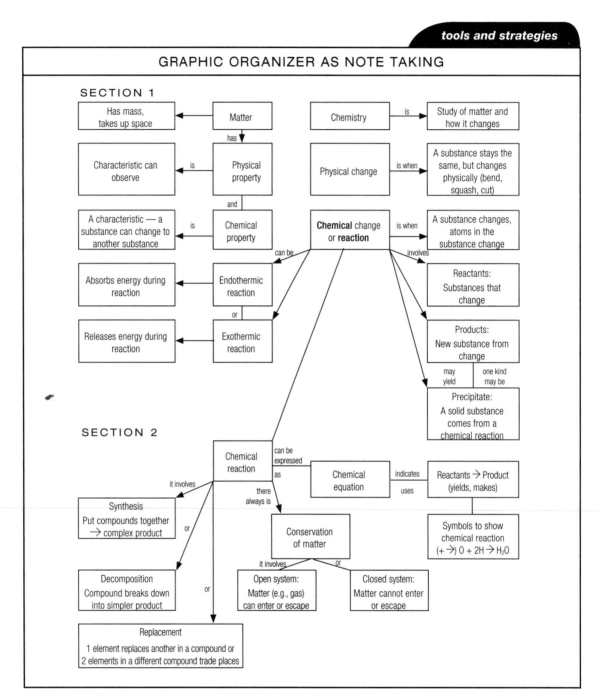

Source: Created by John Carr, based on a physical science textbook intended for eighth grade.

GRAPHIC ORGANIZER:
FLOW MAP OF THE ELEMENTS OF AN EXPOSITORY TEXT

THE GIVER BY LOIS LOWRY

EXPOSITION

Utopia – present day, isolated community governed by Council of Elders.

Rules do not allow making choices, feeling, remembering; people are killed for being unhealthy or breaking rules.

SUPPORTING DETAILS

» Given meals
» Given clothes
» Take medication daily to suppress emotions
» Unhealthy newborns and those too old to be productive are killed by caregivers

RISING ACTION

Twelve-year-old Jonas is Receiver of Memories as lifelong job. He starts to wonder what is better –

» peaceful but mindless life with strict rules, or
» freedom to make good or bad choices, have human feelings and memories.

SUPPORTING DETAILS

» Given meals
» Given clothes
» Take medication daily to suppress emotions
» Unhealthy newborns and those too old to be productive are killed by caregivers

CLIMAX

Jonas decides people should have memories to feel and make choices. Jonas left community so the memories will leave him and go to the people. Jonas plans to return to calm the panicking people.

SUPPORTING DETAILS

» Giver gets weaker as memories enter Jonas
» Giver says he is too old to leave, he will stay and help people until Jonas returns
» Jonas plans to take baby Gabriel so Gabriel won't be killed

FALLING ACTION

Jonas escapes the community with baby Gabriel, and Jonas gets weaker as memories leave his body and return to the community.

SUPPORTING DETAILS

» Airplanes and people try to find Jonas but give up
» The farther Jonas goes, the more memories leave him and the weaker he gets
» He gives Gabriel a few memories to give him energy, to keep him alive

RESOLUTION

Jonas, barely alive, sleds down to a house in another community. It is not clear if Jonas or Gabriel is saved or if Jonas returns to help people adjust to their new life.

SUPPORTING DETAILS

» Houses have Christmas decorations and people inside sharing love
» Jonas is freezing, needs food for energy
» He sleds down a hill, sees people in houses, but is too weak to walk to the nearby house

GRAPHIC ORGANIZER: STORY MAP

Universal Message

Societies need to be governed but maintain basic rights that make us human

Setting

Present day

Utopia — small isolated community

Major Characters

Jonas

Giver

Problem Resolution

Jonas escapes so memories will go to the people and make them feel and think like humans; unsure if he can return to help them not panic

Title

The Giver
by Lois Lowry

Minor Characters

Jonas's family

Turning Point

Jonas decides strict governance is wrong; people need to act human, be free to make choices in life

Major Problem in Story

Council of Elders control everything to maintain tranquility, but citizens no longer act human; act inhuman to those unhealthy

DOUBLE BUBBLE TO COMPARE AND CONTRAST

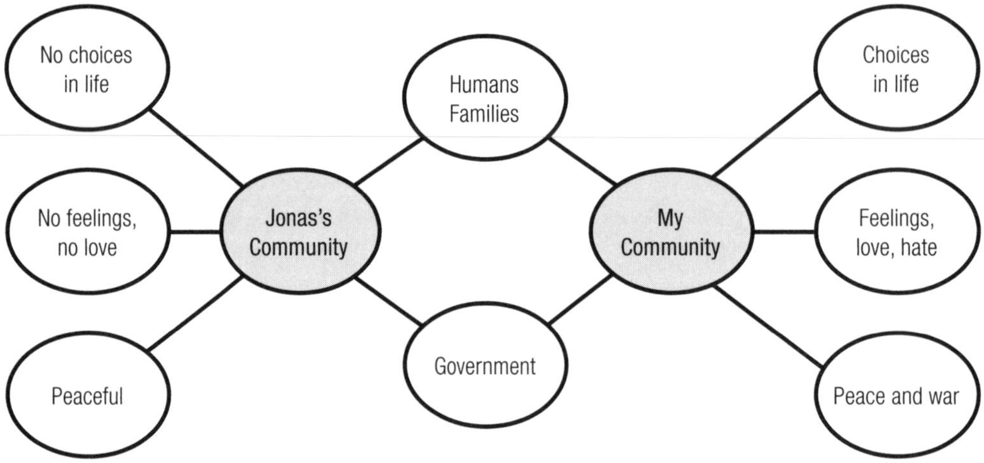

No choices in life

Humans Families

Choices in life

No feelings, no love

Jonas's Community

My Community

Feelings, love, hate

Peaceful

Government

Peace and war

THINK-PAIR-SHARE

Purpose	Think-Pair-Share engages all students simultaneously. It gives students a chance to think about a question, share information with a partner, and consider a peer's point of view in a low-risk situation. This can be especially valuable for English learners, as it structures a way for them to rehearse for whole-class participation. Students are typically more willing to respond in a whole-class conversation after they have had a chance to discuss their ideas with a classmate.
Description	The teacher poses a challenging, open-ended question and gives students a minute or two to think about it and start to formulate an answer. Then, in pairs, students discuss their ideas for one or a few minutes. After the discussion within pairs, the teacher invites partnership reports to the whole class, randomly calls on students, or takes a classroom vote. A variation is for each pair to select one idea or combine ideas/written sentences, share with another pair, and the quad-group selects one idea or combines ideas/written sentences, and then products are shared with the whole class.
Use with English learners and students with learning difficulties	This strategy can be used to apply academic vocabulary, review and summarize what was taught or read, brainstorm ideas, and explore opinions. To protect the opportunity of partners to have equal speaking time, the teacher may want to set time limits and have partners trade speaking and listening roles at a given signal. English learners and students with learning difficulties tend to feel more comfortable discussing their ideas with one or two other students than with the whole class. Anxiety is lowered when giving the group's idea instead of one's own in front of the whole class. This activity also builds meaningful repetition of concepts, which helps English learners process more language and helps students with learning difficulties keep concepts in working memory.
Example	» To begin exploration, students turn to their partners and each offers a prediction about an investigation or develops a concept; the teacher asks pairs to share unique predictions with the whole class. » During data analysis, students analyze charts and graphs and pair-share their interpretations (e.g., "I think this graph means that …"). » At the end of an investigation, students pair-share their conclusions. » Each pair writes two facts from a science text, then quad-groups write the unique facts, and the teacher calls on groups to add facts that prior groups did not mention as the teacher writes the facts on the board.

KWL+

Purpose	This tool serves to get students ready to construct new knowledge, build interest in the topic, and appreciate what they are learning. Student responses help the teacher adjust the lesson to fit students' needs, preconceptions, misconceptions, and interests and to monitor their understanding.
Description	This is a reading-thinking strategy and tool. The teacher writes on a three-column chart students' responses to questions about what they already know (K) about the topic to be studied, what students want (W) to know, and then what they have learned (L) after the reading or lesson. In addition (+), the teacher draws lines or uses a graphic organizer to show connections among the recorded KWL information.
Use with English learners and students with learning difficulties	In advance of the lesson, the teacher can check for individual understanding (K) by asking students to write or otherwise indicate their responses individually before asking for class responses. Any knowledge gaps or misunderstandings that arise will alert the teacher to areas of the lesson needing special attention. Asking what students want to know (W) connects to their personal interests and builds motivation to learn more. Asking what students learned (L) allows them to consolidate their learning and identify gaps in knowledge they still have. Graphically mapping (+) this information, such as drawing lines linking ideas in K with ideas in L, helps to organize and connect ideas in the chart, and this mapping can be especially helpful for students with learning difficulties. The KWL+ chart can be used with English learners at all levels to review, predict, inquire, summarize, and check for understanding.
Examples	The teacher asks, "What do you know about making a bar graph?" and writes students' responses in the "K" column of the KWL chart.
	Then the teacher asks what students want to know about graphing and records what they say in the "W" column. At important points during the lesson, the teacher asks students what they just learned and enters responses in the "L" column. The teacher draws lines to connect old and new information to the inquiry questions and summarizes the connections (+ mapping). The "L" column might incorporate the results of note taking or graphic organizers. Information might be reorganized into categories or as main ideas and supporting details.
	In another example that is specific to scaffolding an assignment with a task worksheet, the teacher reads aloud the information provided on the worksheet, asks students what important information has been provided, and writes appropriate responses in the "K" column of the KWL chart. Next, the teacher reads aloud the procedural instructions on the worksheet, asks students what they want to know, and enters appropriate responses in the "W" column. At the end of the activity, strategies that students used to solve the problem and their answers are entered into the "L" column.

CUES

Purpose   Cues include advance organizers, hints, and questions that are used to focus student thinking and reasoning on pertinent information and help students build bridges among related concepts. Advance organizers and certain questions are always part of a lesson plan, and hints are usually unplanned. All three approaches support students in thinking deeply and making connections among ideas.

Description   **Advance organizers** are one form of cues. They orient students to upcoming important content and activate prior knowledge from a prior lesson or students' lives. Advance organizers form a bridge between what the student already knows and the material that will be taught next. Advance organizers can be embedded in the "K" or "what students already know" part of a KWL+ chart. The teacher identifies certain ideas from the prior lesson and makes a connection to key ideas students will learn in the current lesson. The teacher provides cues that directly frame or preview learning at the start of a lesson. Cues can be a reminder of what information was already presented and how it relates to the new information. They may take the form of an outline, skimming a chapter, or graphic organizers.

Anticipation Guides are a type of advance organizer.[19] The teacher presents a list of main ideas as statements, and students draw on their background knowledge to agree or disagree and give their reasons. The guide of statements and student responses are revisited at key points during or at the end of a lesson. This is an alternative to students generating questions about what they want to know in a KWL+ chart.

Hints are another form of cues. They can be oral questions, brief statements, or affirmations (e.g., "Yes, that's true, but can you explain a little more about …"), or they can be physical, such as hand gestures (e.g., pointing, showing movement) to visually support teacher talk. When students appear to be stumped, the teacher gives a hint to guide their thinking, rather than giving them the expected answer. Implicit corrective feedback during a conversation with an English learner is another type of hint.

Questions also can be a form of cues when the teacher uses questions about what has already been taught to reinforce or check understanding about important information or when modeling procedures, such as predicting and hypothesizing. These questions should not be only about basic factual information; they should also target higher-order, critical thinking skills. These questions may be used to engage students in summarizing, analyzing, making inferences, and other higher-order thinking skills.

Use with English learners and students with learning difficulties   Cues support students with learning difficulties to cognitively process connected information, manipulate it in short-term memory, and store it in long-term memory. Cues support English learners when they are overwhelmed by the English language. Cues are extremely important for many English learners and students with learning difficulties, particularly ASD, for learning tasks that involve relatively abstract concepts, drawing inferences, and organizing information. For example, cues can help students link bits of information about a character that are slowly revealed in a novel and link events with a complex relationship in a social science lesson. The teacher may need to provide cues extensively and in an intense one-to-one or very small group tutoring situation for students with ASD for complex tasks in language arts, science, social science, or mathematics that require higher-order thinking skills (e.g., reasoning, drawing inferences, organizing details into key ideas, organizing objects into categories).

CUES (CONTINUED)

Examples FOR SCIENCE

Animal	Characteristic Organ – Body part	Function Job of body part – What it does
Snake	Two "visual" organs: » 1. Eyes » 2. Heat-sensing pockets near eyes	Two types of "vision": » 1. Eyesight like humans » 2. Detects heat to "see" live objects in the dark
Ant	Antennae	Chemical sensor, similar to smell
Shark	Special long skin band on side of body	Senses electric and magnetic forces, motion, sound, and pressure

During the lesson, the teacher monitors small groups as they conduct experiments, fill in graphic organizers, and answer questions. For groups needing assistance, the teacher asks probing and clarifying questions instead of providing easy answers. For example: What is similar about the sensors of the animals? What is different? Why are they different? What can you conclude from that? What is the connection between environment and sensors?

FOR LANGUAGE ARTS

The teacher assigns students to pairs, identifying each student as "A" or "B," in preparation for reading *The Giver.* As an advance organizer, the teacher gives each pair a chart and directs students A and B to think for 15 seconds about finishing sentence starter 1 and then write a "quick response" in the box in the chart. The teacher then has students take 30 seconds to share their responses and perhaps make revisions. (This is an application of Think-Pair-Share.) The teacher polls some groups to check for understanding before repeating the process for sentence starter 2 and question 3.

	Life X: Peaceful life but no feelings; choices (job, etc.) made for you	Life Y: Joy and sorrow in life, feelings, and you make choices
1. It is good because …	A	B
2. It is bad because …	B	A
3. I/We choose life __ because …		

There is no right or wrong concerning students' answers. The teacher does check that students give specific reasons because they will be expected to identify the main idea and supporting details while reading the story. Before pairs begin working, the teacher might place words such as *peaceful, joy,* and *sorrow* on the wall and ask for definitions if unsure that all students understand the meaning of these key words. The teacher concludes the activity by giving a brief summary of what the story is about.

The teacher guides students to discover the main idea and supporting details at key points while reading the story by using questions and giving hints. Class discussions end with pairs entering information in a graphic organizer as a form of note taking (see Graphic Organizer: Flow Map of the Elements of an Expository Text).

THINK ALOUD

Purpose   The teacher uses Think Aloud to make thinking transparent. Think Aloud can be used to teach comprehension skills, scaffold reading of difficult informational text, and model thought processes in an investigation or exploration. Think Aloud can be used to explicitly connect text and visual concepts and express association, time sequence, and cause and effect. Think Aloud also can be used by students to verbalize their thinking as they present their solution strategies for a task.

Description   The teacher verbalizes his or her own thought processes while considering a question. The teacher models the steps toward answering that question or interpreting and summarizing the solution to the question during a class discussion. The teacher orally models the interactive nature of comprehending a concept and thinking. The teacher gradually fades out the modeling by stopping less often during a lesson to model thinking while fading in opportunities for students to practice thinking aloud.

Think Aloud may be used in conjunction with taking notes or constructing diagrams or graphic organizers. Think Aloud makes "visible" the thinking processes, decisions, connections, and clarifications of actively trying to make meaning. Think Aloud also is a way to model using the lexicon of a discipline before asking students to practice it in their conversations and writing.

Use with English learners and students with learning difficulties   When students use Think Aloud, the teacher may find that students have different perceptions or use alternative solution strategies to approach a question. When students verbalize their thoughts and rationales, the teacher can gain insights into how they think and can identify misconceptions or faulty reasoning and guide students to proper thinking.

Does a student with ASD think in words or pictures? Temple Grandin, a professor with ASD, said she thinks in pictures, organizes them like slides in a carousel, and tries to find the words to describe her pictures to others.

For an English learner, Think Aloud by the teacher might serve as a model of discourse in English to describe one's thinking (e.g., "I think that …" can start a sentence to express an idea or opinion, whereas "I was thinking that …" can be used to express a thought process).

Examples   The teacher draws the structure of the organs and tissues involved in the process of vision. While drawing front and then side views of the eye, the teacher labels each part and then explains the function. The teacher summarizes at certain points, "What I know so far is …" Rather than just explaining the process of vision from the eye to recognition in the brain, the teacher may pose questions or predictions at each step. Sentence Frames may be included to support the teacher's oral questions, answers, and comments. To make the presentation more interactive, the teacher may pose questions and ask students to answer, adjusting explanations to address students' knowledge gaps or misunderstandings.

Teachers also can have students use Think Aloud. By asking a student to say what or how the student is thinking, the teacher attempts to understand what thinking strategy the student uses and whether the student's learning style is verbal ("I say C-A-T over and over to myself"), visual ("I see the letters C-A-T"), tactile ("I use my finger to write the letters on my arm"), spatial ("I see the letters revolving around the head of a cat"), or kinesthetic ("I use my finger to write the letters in the air as I walk around the back of the room").

SUMMARIZATION

Purpose	Summarization helps students understand complex information as they reorganize it for their own purposes. Summarizing can take place when students are engaged in problem solving or investigations, reading a text, or listening to a lecture as they seek to make sense of a body of new information. And because summaries identify key information, they help students review and study for tests.
Description	Summarizations are typically complex and extensive, connecting details to a concept and a concept to other concepts. To effectively summarize information, the student must recognize the main ideas, the expendable details, the illuminating details, and the academic language that is a crucial aspect of communicating the content. Restated as a step-by-step process, "students must delete some information, substitute some information, keep some information," and then demonstrate comprehension by stating important information using their own words.[20] The summary could range from notes that the student will use to review to a composition that culminates a research project.
	The teacher models and guides as students practice comprehending information and progress from very brief summary statements of short text passages to full summaries of a full text or other body of information. The "L" in the KWL+ strategy might contain a very brief summary or discrete concepts. To explicitly teach the skill of summarization, the teacher might use Think Aloud to model the thinking process involved in summarization while reading a text. To support the Think Aloud visually, the teacher displays a text passage, crosses out phrases or sentences that should be deleted, writes substitute statements between lines or margins, and might circle or highlight what is kept. The teacher uses Think-Pair-Share as a scaffold for practicing summarization until students have sufficient skills to summarize independently. In Think-Pair-Share, pairs or trios compare what they deleted, substituted, and kept; then they "take the best" and write a brief summary. The teacher might have groups share at two points in the process: after selecting important information and then after writing the summary.
	Note taking is closely related to summarizing, since to take effective notes, a student must determine what is most important and then state the information succinctly in a way that will convey meaning for future use and review. The teacher also might use Think Aloud to model the thinking process for taking notes using a graphic organizer or Sentence Frames. After deleting, substituting, and keeping information in a text, the teacher uses Think Aloud to model the thinking process of selecting a type of graphic organizer appropriate for the purpose of reading the text and the alternative traditional outline format. Students use the notes in the graphic organizer or outline to express a summary orally or in writing in full, connected sentences and paragraphs.
Use for English learners and students with learning difficulties	Summarization at each chunk of new information helps students perform a mental task of moving meaningful chunks to long-term memory.
	English learners, particularly at the lower levels, likely will need scaffolds such as Sentence Frames, graphic organizers, and illustrations to accompany words. It may be helpful for English learners and students with learning difficulties to complete summaries and notes as members of small groups, as discussed in the description above.

SUMMARIZATION (CONTINUED)

Example Following is an example of deleting and keeping important information in a passage with the purpose of defining summarization and identifying two strategies the teacher uses to scaffold the process.

> Summarizations are typically complex and extensive, connecting details to a concept and a concept to other concepts. ~~To effectively summarize information, the student must recognize the main ideas, the expendable details, the illuminating details, and the academic language that is a crucial aspect of communicating the content. Restated as a step-by-step process,~~ "students must delete some information, substitute some information, keep some information," and then demonstrate comprehension by stating important information using their own words. ~~The summary could range from notes that the student will use to review to a composition that culminates a research project.~~

> The teacher models and guides as students practice comprehending information and progress from very brief summary statements of short text passages to full summaries of a full text or other body of information. ~~The "L" in the KWL+ strategy might contain a very brief summary or discrete concepts. To explicitly teach the skill of summarization,~~ the teacher might use Think Aloud to model the thinking process involved in summarization while reading a text. To support the Think Aloud visually, the teacher displays a text passage, crosses out phrases or sentences that should be deleted, writes substitute statements between lines or margins, and might circle or highlight what is kept. ~~The teacher uses Think-Pair-Share as a scaffold for practicing summarization until students have sufficient skills to summarize independently.~~ In Think-Pair-Share, pairs or trios compare what they deleted, substituted, and kept; then they "take the best" and write a brief summary. ~~The teacher might have groups share at two points in the process: after selecting important information and then after writing the summary.~~

Following is a simple example of part of a response form with Sentence Frames to scaffold English learners and students with learning difficulties in an inclusive middle school biology classroom to demonstrate comprehension and summarization. The teacher distributes the response form and gives direction for trios to read the textbook section and agree on responses to fill in the blanks. Before students begin reading, the teacher asks students to identify key words in the response form that could be clues for finding answers in the text as a reading for comprehension strategy. The teacher tells students they cannot copy definitions; they must use their own words to demonstrate comprehension. As trios read and fill in the response form, the teacher monitors groups, providing hints and asking guiding questions as needed.

> There are two main causes of variation in a population:
>
> 1. Mutation, which means _____
>
>   _____
>
>   - Sometimes the new protein _____
>   - Mutations can be caused when DNA is _____ during replication, by mistakes during meiosis or by radiation or chemicals.
>
> 2. Recombination, which means _____
>
>   _____
>
>   - Since each parent gives only half (½) of his or her DNA to the child,
>
>   _____

ENDNOTES FOR CHAPTER 5

[1] The term *scaffolding* was first used to describe parent-child talk by Wood, D. J., Bruner, J., & Ross, G. (1976). The role of tutoring in problem solving. *Journal of Child Psychology and Psychiatry, 17*(2), 89–100.

[2] Scaffolding is discussed widely in education literature. The following sources are particularly germane to this presentation of scaffolding mathematics instruction for English learners: Coggins, D., Kravin, D., Coates, G. D., & Carroll, M. D. (2007). *English language learners in the mathematics classroom.* Thousand Oaks, CA: Corwin Press; Ellis, E. S., & Worthington, L. A. (2004). *Research synthesis on effective teaching principles and the design of quality tools for educators.* Eugene, OR: National Center to Improve the Tools of Educators, University of Oregon. Retrieved from http://www.iu17.org/393999727151823/lib/393999727151823/Effective%20Teaching.pdf; Freeman, D., & Freeman, Y. (1988). *Sheltered English instruction* (ERIC Digest, ED301070). Washington, DC: ERIC Clearinghouse on Languages and Linguistics. Retrieved from http://www.ericdigests.org/pre-9210/english.htm; Gibbons, P. (2002). *Scaffolding language, scaffolding learning: Teaching second language learners in the mainstream classroom.* Portsmouth, NH: Heinemann; National Clearinghouse on Bilingual Education. (1987). Sheltered English: An approach to content area instruction for limited-English-proficient students. *Forum, 10*(6), 1–3; Vygotsky, L. (1986). *Thought and language* (A. Kozulin, Ed. and Trans.). Cambridge, MA: Harvard University Press.

[3] Gibbons, P. (2002).

[4] Marzano, R. J., Pickering, D. J., & Pollock, J. E. (2001). *Classroom instruction that works: Research-based strategies for increasing student achievement.* Alexandria, VA: Association for Supervision and Curriculum Development; California Department of Education. (2000). *Strategic teaching and learning: Standards-based instruction to promote content literacy in grades four through twelve.* Sacramento: California Department of Education Press.

[5] California Department of Education. (2010). *Improving education for English learners: Research-based approaches.* Sacramento: California Department of Education; Herrell, A. L., & Jordan, M. L. (2003). *Fifty strategies for teaching English language learners.* Englewood Cliffs, NJ: Prentice Hall; Hill, J. D., & Flynn, K. M. (2006). *Classroom instruction that works for English language learners.* Alexandria, VA: Association for Supervision and Curriculum Development.

[6] Scruggs, T. E., Mastropieri, M. A., Berkeley, S., & Graetz, J. E. (2009). Do special education interventions improve learning of secondary content? A meta-analysis. *Remedial & Special Education, 31*(6), 437–449. A summary can be retrieved from http://nichcy.org/research/summaries/abstract80; Winebrenner, S. (2006). *Teaching kids with learning difficulties in the regular classroom.* Minneapolis, MN: Free Spirit Publishing.

[7] Marzano, R. J., Pickering, D. J., & Pollock, J. E. (2001).

[8] Albus, D., Thurlow, M., & Clapper, A. (2007). *Standards-based instructional strategies for English language learners with disabilities* (ELLs with Disabilities Report 18). Minneapolis: University of Minnesota, National Center on Educational Outcomes.

[9] We follow the lead of Marzano, Pickering, and Pollock (2001), which includes note taking as a type of summarization.

[10] No research studies have been published that explored the combined effect of these six strategies on student achievement, so the authors posit that there *might* be a synergistic effect.

[11] Curwin, R. L., Mendler, A. N., & Mendler, B. D. (2008). *Discipline with dignity* (3rd ed.). Alexandria, VA: Association for Supervision and Curriculum Development. See pp. 21–24.

[12] See http://www.wested.org/ReadingApprenticeship

[13] Bremer, C. D., Vaughn, S., Clapper, A. T., & Kim, A-H. (2002). Collaborative strategic reading (CSR): Improving secondary students' reading comprehension skills. *NCSET Research to Practice Brief, 1*(2). Retrieved from http://www.ncset.org/publications/viewdesc.asp?id=424

[14] Schoenbach, R., Greenleaf, C. L., Cziko, C., & Hurwitz, L. (1999). *Reading for understanding: A guide to improving reading in middle and high school classrooms.* San Francisco: Jossey-Bass.

[15] Guskey, T. R. (2000). *Evaluating professional development.* Thousand Oaks, CA: Corwin Press.

[16] These thinking maps can be found at ThinkingMaps.com, along with examples and support workshops. Inspiration.com and Kidspiration.com provide drawing tools and examples.

[17] Hyerle, D. (1996). *Visual tools for constructing knowledge.* Alexandria, VA: Association for Supervision and Curriculum Development; Hall, T., & Strangman, N. (2002). *Graphic organizers.* Wakefield, MA: National Center on Accessing the General Curriculum. Retrieved from http://aim.cast.org/learn/historyarchive/backgroundpapers/graphic_organizers

[18] Adapted from Winebrenner, S. (2006).

[19] For a full description of Anticipation Guides, see http://olc.spsd.sk.ca/DE/PD/instr/strats/anticiguide/index.htm or http://www.indiana.edu/~l517/anticipation_guides.htm, which includes a high school example.

[20] Marzano, R. J., Pickering, D. J., & Pollock, J. E. (2001). See p. 30. In the chapter on summarization, the authors give examples of summary frames for different types of information, such as narrative, definition, argumentation, and problem/solution.

CHAPTER 6

Strategies for Scaffolding Classroom Assessments

The aim of assessment is primarily to *educate* and *improve* student performance, not merely to *audit* it.

— Grant Wiggins

Teachers who focus on giving English learners and students with learning difficulties equal access to the curriculum will also want to make sure that these students have a fair and accurate way to communicate what they are learning. Providing equal opportunity means scaffolding assessments so that diverse learners can comprehend what is being asked and scaffolding oral or written responses in order to support students in expressing their understanding of the concepts and skills being assessed. Alternative assessments and scaffolding strategies can support English learners, students with learning difficulties, and other diverse learners in expressing their ideas and show their actual achievement orally or in writing.[1]

In this chapter, we discuss scaffolding strategies that assessment experts generally refer to as *accommodations*. We stick with the term *scaffolding* in order to keep nomenclature simple and consistent in this book and because some of the strategies in this chapter for scaffolding assessments are also presented in chapter 5 for scaffolding learning. We consider only tests in English, not tests translated into a student's native language. Translating a test does not ensure comparability, especially when certain concepts do not exist or are much more difficult to state in a language other than English. An English learner taught in English-only content classes may perform higher on a test in English than in the student's native language; consider a high school English learner who left Mexico in sixth grade with no opportunities to continue education in the Spanish language. Also, many teachers speak only English, so they cannot directly administer and score assessments in another language. Thus, this book focuses on the majority of classroom situations.

This chapter discusses how to create or select, modify, and administer fair and useful classroom assessments that inform a teacher about diverse learners' understanding of the content. These strategies do not apply to state assessments, although states do specify accommodations and alternative assessments. The information in this chapter could be used to review the extent to which district-mandated assessments meet diverse students' needs and are culturally sensitive or unbiased.

Not only does it take a variety of ways to teach English learners and students with learning difficulties, but it also takes a variety of ways for these students to show what they have learned. The scaffolding strategies for classroom assessments offer alternative ways for particular students to accurately show what they know; at the same time, these strategies maintain high expectations regarding the same content standards for all students.

One purpose of classroom assessments is to give students rapid feedback about what they have learned so they can take responsibility for planning what they need to learn. A second purpose is for teachers to have the most current evidence of student progress in order to reflect on teaching practices and plan future lessons. A key component of Response to Intervention is monitoring student progress and using data to inform decisions about what is and is not working for each student.

TEST BIAS

One kind of test bias is cultural bias. When a test item requires or favors knowledge about information related to a particular culture, it is said to have a cultural bias in favor of a student with that cultural background and against a student with a different cultural background.

Imagine the following is a mathematics test item on England's national assessment:

> In a five-day match in test cricket, Team A makes 250 runs at the end of the first inning and takes the option to make Team B bat again. How many runs did Team B score in the first inning?

To solve this item, a student needs to know how to subtract numbers and solve inequalities. The student also needs to be familiar enough with the rules of cricket to know that Team A must have at least 200 runs more than Team B at the end of the first inning in order to have the option of making Team B bat again. The test item is culturally biased in favor of students who have lived all their lives in England or in another place where cricket is a popular sport. Any student taking this test who had recently moved to England from, for example, the United States, would be likely not to have the cultural background knowledge to solve this problem and might wish that this was a multiple choice item in order to have a chance at a wild guess.

Similarly, imagine that the following is a mathematics test item in the United States:

> Suppose the San Francisco Giants scored 9 runs in a regulation game. What is the average number of runs the Giants scored per inning?

In this case, a student who is an avid fan of baseball would readily know to divide 9 runs by 9 innings to get the answer of 1 run per inning. But any student who has never been exposed to or interested in baseball may have no idea that there are 9 innings in a regulation game and so would be unable to correctly answer this test item.

In general, English learners who have not lived in the United States for very long are not likely to have the vocabulary or cultural knowledge of native English speakers. Test bias can be extended from items that favor one culture over others to bias in terms of ethnicity/race, gender, and personal prior nonschool experiences and interests. When a test item contains or assumes knowledge of a topic or vocabulary that has not been taught, that item is biased in favor of the student who has that contextual knowledge. A simple rule of thumb is to create assessment items in which all of the information and all of the vocabulary in the item were previously taught to all students taking the test. The teacher should review existing assessments for classroom use (e.g., curriculum-based) for possible bias.

The teacher who knows key personal information about individual students – their knowledge, experiences, and interests outside of school – is more likely to notice biased items than the teacher who knows very little about the personal lives of the students.

CLASSROOM ASSESSMENT

There are two types of classroom assessments: formative and summative. *Formative assessments* are used at the start of, during, and/or at the end of a day's instruction, and they provide feedback that (a) helps the teacher make adjustments to the lesson and (b) increases the students' awareness of what they did or did not understand. *Summative assessments* are given at the end of a unit of study, and the results help the teacher to decide the overall approach for the next unit and assign course grades.

Formative Assessment

Formative assessment can be a powerful teaching tool when teachers use the results to adjust their instructional strategies to reach all students in the classroom.[2] As Benjamin Bloom found in an experimental study of a mathematics unit lesson, teachers making instructional adjustments based on formative assessment dramatically narrowed the range of student achievement, and the average student outperformed 84 percent of students in traditional classrooms where the teachers did not use formative assessments or make instructional adjustments (see Figure 6.1).[3] In other words, when teachers take the time to assess during the teaching process and use the feedback to make midcourse adjustments, the process can result in more students mastering the lesson content. Researcher Thomas Guskey suggests that adjustments are effective when they present concepts differently, when corrective activities are different and appropriate for different learning styles, and when students are and feel more successful as a result of the corrective activities.[4]

The effective teacher uses a few quick and easy methods to survey which students do and do not understand the content during the course of a lesson and then tries different approaches as needed. Just as an ounce of prevention is worth a pound of cure, noticing early failures to comprehend key ideas and adjusting a lesson to fit student needs can prevent many failures at the end of the unit of study.

Scores or other information from formative assessments should not be part of a student's course grade; during a lesson students should feel they can convey what they are thinking with no risk.[5]

We do not recommend asking students, "Do you understand?" or using similar questions that beg a "yes" response. Instead, we suggest asking a question that requires a student to state an idea or repeat the teacher's directions (e.g., "What are you going to do in your small group?"). When the teacher asks questions of individual students in the context of a whole-class lesson, it is useful to make two practices a habit: (a) waiting at least five seconds for all students to think about the question and their answer, and (b) walking close to individual English learners and students with learning difficulties and asking the question (or repeating it). Being in close proximity, the student will likely feel more comfortable responding

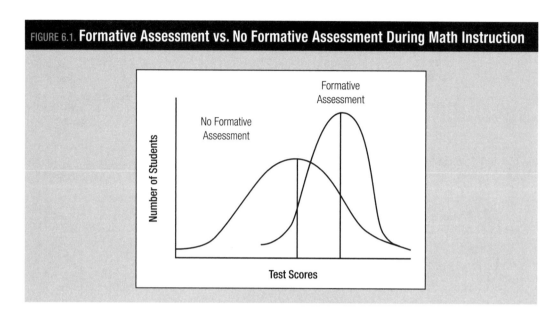

FIGURE 6.1. Formative Assessment vs. No Formative Assessment During Math Instruction

to the teacher than "in front of the whole class." Also, some students with learning difficulties who are hypersensitive to sound may have difficulty attending to the teacher's voice if far away and if nearby noises are competing for the student's attention.

Here are four techniques to check for understanding of all students at the same time:

» Hand gestures, such as thumbs up (I agree, yes), thumbs to the side (I politely disagree, no), and flat hand (I do not understand the question or comment).

» Color-coded cards indicating agree, disagree, don't understand, or another answer choice.

» Whiteboards on which each student quickly illustrates or writes a brief answer. Then, when directed to do so, all students hold their whiteboards up for the teacher to see.

» "Ticket Out" — on a slip of paper or in a journal, students write a brief response, such as what they learned, what was confusing, or what was most interesting at the end of the day's lesson.

These techniques can be used to respond to what the teacher or another student says. Asking all students to quickly show agreement or disagreement with another student's answer or comment engages all students in listening critically to one another and widens the conversation from teacher-student to teacher-student-students. Students easily adapt to these techniques. The process is both fast and comfortable, and the teacher can take immediate action based on what the students reveal. For example, when many students signal confusion about a concept, this indicates to the teacher the need to take a different approach; if a smaller group of students signals that they do not understand, the teacher may convene them for more specific instruction while other students move into an independent activity.

Monitoring students while they are working individually or in small groups is another way to check the understanding of some students, since the teacher cannot monitor all students at once nor get around to all groups when one or two particular groups need significant time. The teacher is able to observe and provide cues to guide individual students or small groups in their learning activities. When many students are confused, the teacher may stop the group or individual work and conduct direct instruction in a different way than initially presented to clarify concepts or the learning activity itself. This is what makes a good teacher really effective — planning a good lesson and then enhancing it during instruction.

Checking for understanding not only helps the teacher adjust a lesson, but also provides feedback to students about what they do know and what they need to learn. Getting informative feedback from the teacher throughout a lesson helps students assume control and responsibility for their learning and adjust learning as needed.[6] The teacher can include feedback about English language conventions for English learners and about verbal expression for students with language difficulties while checking for understanding. For example, if an English learner responds, "Octagon have eight side," the teacher can provide implicit corrective feedback while acknowledging the correct mathematics answer: "Yes, an octagon has eight sides." This can occur orally or in writing, depending on whether the student is speaking or writing answers.

Summative Assessment

Assessing students at the end of a study unit or chapter — summative assessment — informs the teacher and students of final levels of accomplishment and allows the teacher to analyze results for groups of students as well as for individuals. Information about which content was challenging for each student informs the teacher's decisions about how to modify the teaching strategies and activities for the next lesson and whether to offer program interventions, such as tutoring.

But how can the teacher greatly improve learning during the unit? The National Research Council frames classroom assessment as the process of teaching scientifically:

> Teachers collect information about students' understanding almost continuously and make adjustments to their teaching on the basis of their interpretation of that information. They observe critical incidents in the classroom, formulate hypotheses about the causes of those incidents, question students to test their hypotheses, interpret students' responses, and adjust their teaching plans.[7]

In these terms, assessment allows the teacher to treat each lesson as an experiment: predicting that certain strategies and activities will help students learn rigorous content; monitoring the effects of the lesson on student engagement and achievement; and analyzing the assessment data to make conclusions about teaching practices and materials.

The teacher must examine assessments in the course's main text and determine if they are appropriate for the teacher's particular students, especially the English learners, students with learning difficulties, and other students who struggle with comprehending what they read and with expressing their ideas in writing.

TYPES OF ASSESSMENT INSTRUMENTS

Cloze Tests and Sentence Frames

Cloze tests are similar to Sentence Frames. They require students to fill in the blanks in sentences with one or perhaps a few words, which might be appropriate for an English learner at the Entering level of English language proficiency (e.g., "A quadrilateral has ___ sides"). Sentence Frames allow longer responses (e.g., "The main idea is ..."; "Whales are ____ because ...") and generally are more suited to the level of support needed by English learners above the Entering level and students with learning difficulties. The student might have the option of writing, typing, or responding orally for Cloze tests and Sentence Frames. The purpose is to provide students with a scaffold as long as they need it to express what they know. To maintain the rigor of content knowledge, the teacher must avoid giving hints and ensure that this type of assessment instrument maintains the kind or level of critical thinking expected of other students who have higher English literacy skills.[8] A word bank may be provided, but it should include extra words and/or allow for words to be used more than once. The point is to reduce student guessing so that the teacher is fairly certain of what students do and do not know.

Multiple-Choice Tests

Multiple-choice tests can be very difficult for English learners and students with learning difficulties because the test items are typically very succinct — with little context to help these students and other struggling readers figure out what an item means. Teachers may need to provide support by rephrasing and including context clues for certain test items. All students can benefit from covering the answer choices, reading the question, thinking of an answer, and then looking for a similar answer choice. Suggested supports include:

» Spend a little time teaching test-taking skills, particularly related to the content area. If some test items require students to pick the "best" answer, ensure that students understand and have had experience with this type of item. Let them know that there may be answers that are partially correct but just not as good as the "most correct" or "best" answer.

» Limit the number of items, especially items with long statements, to avoid student fatigue — English learners and students with learning difficulties may prefer open-ended questions instead of slogging through four options for each of many multiple-choice questions.

» Eliminate items with answer choices such as "None of the above" and "A and B" to avoid confusion and cognitive overload.

» Make sure item stems and answer choices are written in the simplest, most straightforward wording possible. Highlight key words (bold, underline, or all capital letters), particularly negatives such as "not," so students do not miss them. Test developers can fall into the trap of devising convoluted statements in order to keep a question very succinct and all response choices nearly the same length. For a teacher creating a classroom assessment, having response choices with similar lengths is not nearly as important as having wording that is easy to understand.

For multiple-choice tests that base items on illustrations, graphs, or tables, the following tips are helpful for all learners.[9]

» Make sure illustrations are accurate and clear and include appropriate scales when relevant.

» Use the same illustration as a reference for multiple questions. English learners will benefit from the familiar context.

» Be sure the labels on the illustration match those embedded in item prompts.

» Limit the steps necessary to interpret information from an illustration, graph, or table.

» When possible, select contexts that are familiar to students or that relate to their backgrounds and experiences.

Short-Answer Tests

—evaluates what level can they write to

Students can respond orally or in writing to test items calling for a phrase or up to a few sentences. When applicable, students may be encouraged to draw illustrations or to create or fill in simple graphic organizers (e.g., to show relationships among polygons), organizing their thoughts before answering aloud or in writing. Short-answer tests can be structured to provide Sentence Starters and function words to connect ideas for students who need a writing scaffold.

Written Performance Tasks

These tasks require more than a few sentences and can range from several paragraphs to full-length papers, including research reports, essays, and expository, narrative, and persuasive compositions. The writing that students do in different disciplines varies across type, purpose, and product. For example, students may write expository, descriptive, analytic, and technical responses or reports. They write for purposes such as exemplifying, describing phenomena, raising questions, clarifying, and supporting ideas. And they create different products, such as notes, portfolios, data charts, reports, essays, and logs.

To demonstrate their knowledge in writing, students need explicit teaching about the purpose and form of each type of writing. Such instruction by the content area teacher can be supported with collaboration from the English language arts, ELD/ESL, or special education teacher. For all students, models should be a key feature of writing instruction. Models should be discussed with students and available for them to investigate and refer to. Graphic organizers can be used to help students make visual sense of their thinking. Word Walls might also be readily available to English learners and certain students with learning difficulties (e.g., visual-spatial thinkers who cogitate in pictures, not words). Refer to the writing skills in the academic language charts in chapter 3 as a guide to what can be expected of English learners at different English language proficiency levels. English learners can be expected to progress from writing a few words in the primary grades and a few simple sentences in middle and high school to writing multiparagraph compositions with very few errors of conventions at the highest English language proficiency level (Bridging). Sentence Frames or other prompts can scaffold English learners at levels between Entering and Bridging and many students with learning difficulties. Starting with a graphic organizer helps both English learners and students with learning difficulties "see" the concepts and connections that they will put into connected sentences.

Students may be offered choices of other types of performance assessments, such as performing a play, constructing a model bridge that applies mathematical concepts, and creating and delivering a lesson to students at a lower grade level. However, the alternative tasks must be as rigorous as the types of assessments discussed above. Providing flexible means to learn skills and to demonstrate mastery of them is highly motivating for students. It honors learner diversity and encourages creativity and innovative thinking.

Oral Presentations

The general education teacher needs to consider whether it is appropriate for English learners at the Entering and Emerging levels and many students with learning difficulties to present formal oral reports in general education classrooms. These students may feel too anxious trying to express themselves in front of the whole class and may not yet have sufficient language skills to clearly express their ideas. *They* might give oral presentations with teacher support (e.g., prompting, rephrasing to achieve a coherent response) if the students agree and the classroom climate is risk-free and supportive. The student might orally present just to the teacher or to a small group of respectful peers. Multimedia and use of technology such as PowerPoint, where visuals are blended with brief text, can support students as they orally present their reports.

STRATEGIES TO SCAFFOLD ASSESSMENTS FOR ENGLISH LEARNERS AND STUDENTS WITH LEARNING DIFFICULTIES

Scaffolding strategies are meant to elicit the most accurate information about what students know and can do, without giving them an unfair advantage over students who do not need these scaffolds. All students have diverse strengths as learners and as test takers. Some may have pronounced learning strengths in certain modalities, such as visual or aural, or they may have assessment preferences that influence their ability to show what they truly know. For English learners, an additional consideration is the challenge they face to perform in English. The more alternatives (e.g., multiple choice, written and oral short answer, portfolio of key student work), the more accurate the test results are likely to be for a range of students.

Figure 6.2 describes common scaffolding strategies that teachers may use in their classrooms to assess English learners and other students. (These strategies are for testing that is in English only.) Some strategies address how a test is administered; others address the test instrument and task options. The closer an English learner is to the Entering level of English language proficiency, the more scaffolding of the student's interaction with the test is necessary to yield accurate results.

FIGURE 6.2. Assessment Scaffolding Strategies for Diverse Students

Strategy	Purpose or Use
Extra Time	Provide extra time for struggling readers to read and understand test questions. English learners and some students with learning difficulties have extra thinking to do simply to understand and respond to a question in English.
Word Walls, Glossaries	Provide Word Walls created during instruction for reference during assessment so English learners and students with learning difficulties can more easily communicate conceptual thinking. Allow English learners at appropriate levels to use glossaries (except when testing vocabulary, of course).
Notes in Primary Language	When students are allowed to use notes during an assessment, allow English learners to refer to notes they made in their primary language. This makes it more likely that students can produce, in English, answers that they know in their primary language.
Models and Rubrics	Provide models of expected student work, particularly for students who have not previously produced this kind of product. Preview the scoring guide or rubric that will be used to judge the work. Previewing models and explaining rubrics before or during instruction helps students understand lesson and assessment objectives.

Strategy	Purpose or Use
Revised Test Directions or Items	Some test directions can be much more difficult to understand than the concepts measured. Revise test directions and item contents to reduce linguistic complexity. Read directions aloud and rephrase them as necessary to be sure English learners and certain students with learning difficulties know what they are expected to do. Simplify test directions as much as possible. For example, segment multistep directions and break steps into ministeps if possible, stating one step at a time and allowing for student responses between steps. When responses cannot be segmented, have students use the written directions (perhaps supported with illustrations or picture-symbols) as a checklist for reviewing that they have completed all parts of the task. Ensure that students encounter in a test the same key words and phrases that were used during instruction. Increase students' opportunity to understand the questions by providing synonyms or additional context for key ideas.
Oral Responses	Communicating through writing can be very challenging for English learners and some students with learning difficulties, especially when anxiety is high during an assessment. Allow novice English learners to give oral responses while the rest of the class completes a written test. (Out of range of the rest of the class, prompt students individually and scaffold the conversation as necessary to elicit meaningful responses.) Provide Sentence Frames for students who need support with open-ended questions and ask them to attempt written answers; then prompt students orally to give them an opportunity to clarify written answers that are ambiguous or confusing.
Illustrations, Graphic Organizers	Allow students to express ideas first with labeled drawings, diagrams, or graphic organizers. Then follow up by asking students to give oral explanations, written open-ended responses, or demonstrations.
Hands-on Activities	Have students perform a demonstration, activity, or investigation and describe or explain their actions and thinking processes. For example, students might cycle through various assessment task stations in the classroom, responding to the problem or question posed at each station. For students who can write brief answers, have them do so, and orally prompt English learners as needed.
Language Conventions	Ignore errors in language conventions in order to focus on students' understanding of content when the target is not about language convention standards. The time for corrective feedback of oral or written responses is during instruction. Expect Entering and Emerging English learners to make many errors as they struggle to communicate meaning.
Small Groups	Administer a test separately, rephrasing directions as needed, to a small group of English learners and students with learning difficulties if it helps to lower their anxiety. Small groups should not discuss answers or hear each others' answers; students must independently complete the test for accurate individual results.

Source: Adapted from Carr, J., Sexton, U., & Lagunoff, R. (2007). *Making science accessible to English learners: A guidebook for teachers.* San Francisco: WestEd.

When revising test directions or items, the syntax can be revised to reduce complexity (and still measure students' knowledge of the construct at the same level of difficulty), and vocabulary can be changed without dumbing down the content. Ensuring that key vocabulary and syntax of test directions and items are taught and practiced during instruction avoids oversimplifying test language. For example, during testing

Practice Interpreting Points

Presenting and comparing data is an important use of the coordinate plane. For example, the doctor's office is one place where comparing data can be helpful.

The graph below compares the number of heartbeats per minute to the number of breaths per minute.

1. What is the independent variable?

   (a) Heartbeats
   (b) Breaths
   (c) Minutes

Remember, in math we put the independent variable on the x-axis.

2. What is the dependent variable?

   (a) Heartbeats
   (b) Breaths
   (c) Minutes

3. Explain or interpret the meaning of each point plotted on the grid.

   Point A, (75, 12):

   Point B, (130, 20):

   Point C, (175, 28):

4. How do you think hearbeats per minute and breaths per minute are related?

Source: Presented with permission of WestEd and It's About Time; appears in the *Aim for Algebra* program. Retrieved from http://www.its-about-time.com/aim/aim.html

a teacher can ask for "synonyms" instead of "words with the same meaning" as long as students have become quite familiar with the word *synonym* during instruction. Teachers need to ensure their students are familiar with all vocabulary on tests, not just key terms. When contextual wording is used in test items, teachers should consider changing less culturally familiar words and phrases to words and phrases that reflect more familiar cultural experiences (e.g., from "fish in an aquarium" to "students on the playground" for students who have no knowledge of an aquarium, assuming the aquarium or playground is just context for getting at the tested skill, such as asking students to add or subtract).

The particular strategies the teacher decides to use with diverse students will vary by the type of assessment, as well as by the students' level of English language proficiency. Figure 6.3 is an example of a written mathematics assessment that gives all students an opportunity to express their understanding at varying levels of language development. The assessment content is aligned with content standards relating to points on a coordinate plane.

The assessment could be modified to include more support for certain students. Such support might include:

>   Rephrasing the directions for item 3 (e.g., "Explain using words what point A (75, 12) means")

>   Providing an example response for item 3 (e.g., "If your heart is beating 50 times per minute, then you are taking 8 breaths per minute")

>   Providing Sentence Frames for items 3 and 4 (e.g., "If your heart is beating __ times **per minute**, then you are taking ___ breaths per minute")

>   Prompting English learners to respond orally

>   Creating a Word Wall that includes key vocabulary during instruction (e.g., *graph, compare, variable, point, per minute, related, independent, dependent, beating, breaths*)

INTEGRATING INSTRUCTION AND ASSESSMENT

In standards-based lesson planning, also called *backwards mapping,* the teacher first selects specific content standards as the lesson objectives, choosing a few of the most important or essential standards to discuss with students so they know to focus on these, although the lesson may make connections to other standards as well.[10]

Second, the teacher selects a good assessment that emphasizes those essential standards and then builds in scaffolding strategies for students who need them. The teacher is aware of the test format and of the vocabulary, knowledge, and skills required to answer the questions and follow the test directions. If possible, the teacher plans to offer alternative assessments, knowing that diverse learners also prefer diverse ways to show what they have learned. The teacher asks several questions when evaluating an assessment:

>   Does the assessment truly measure rigorous standards?

>   What will proficient performance on this assessment look like?

>   Do the scaffolding strategies really measure the content standards at a reasonable level of rigor, similar to that required of other students?

Third, the teacher plans learning activities so that all students have equal opportunity to learn the content and practice the skills. Equal opportunity means that diverse learning activities are presented to students because they have diverse styles, interests, and levels of learning. Visual learners, for example, have graphic organizers and other visual means to access content, but they also experience other modalities so that they become well-rounded learners and appreciate a variety of styles within the classroom. Reading materials are geared to students' various reading levels. Students are able to choose from alternative tasks, which lead them to become more responsible for their own learning. In selecting the learning activities, the teacher reflects on each and asks whether it helps students understand the essential standards and whether it prepares them for the assessment.

Fourth, the teacher plans instructional strategies and scaffolds (see chapter 5 for examples) for students who need them in order to be successful during the learning activities. Instruction is multimodal, perhaps focusing on a particular mode at one time and reviewing what was learned by focusing on another mode. Multimodality supports varied student interests and skills.

Last, the teacher connects the dots by reviewing the entire unit lesson plan. What is taught is assessed. There must be a clear connection among the standards, assessment, student activities, and teaching strategies. If not, the teacher amends the lesson plan. During instruction, the teacher uses frequent formative assessments, checking for understanding and using the feedback to quickly adjust the lesson and try other strategies.

SHARING RESULTS AND IDEAS

A teacher can learn much from assessments or test results but still miss some things or not know how to help some students who are struggling. Collaborating with other teachers to evaluate student work or analyze test results can enhance both student and teacher learning.[11] This professional activity is called *data team meetings* in some school districts.

The shared evaluation of student work might start with a trusted colleague and expand to departmental study teams. These sessions enable teachers to become more skilled at evaluating student work by giving them the opportunity to review and analyze a larger sample of work than that of their own students. By sharing results, teachers can also evaluate their individual instruction practices and assessments in comparison with those of their peers.

While analyzing student results together, collaborating teachers also consider what they might do better the next time. They take a hard look at the results for lower-scoring students to determine whether the test was accurate and fair for these students. They also explore different teaching strategies and learning activities that might better help these students as a group, and they share insights about individual students. This kind of embedded professional development is highly relevant to teachers and can produce valuable results for students.

ENDNOTES FOR CHAPTER 6

[1] Trumbull, E., & Farr, B. (2005). *Language and learning: What teachers need to know.* Norwood, MA: Christopher-Gordon. See chapter 7, Language and Assessment.

[2] Black, P., & William, D. (1998). Inside the black box: Raising standards through classroom assessment. *Phi Delta Kappan, 80*(2), 139–149. Retrieved from http://www.pdkintl.org/kappan/kbla9810.htm; Chappuis, S., & Chappuis, J. (2007/2008). The best value in formative assessment. *Educational Leadership, 65*(4), 14–19; Fisher, D., & Frey, N. (2007). *Checking for understanding: Formative assessment techniques for your classroom.* Alexandria, VA: Association for Supervision and Curriculum Development.

[3] Bloom, B. (1984). The 2 sigma problem: The search for methods of group instruction as effective as one-to-one tutoring. *Educational Researcher, 13*(6), 4–16. Retrieved from http://dlsystems.us/readings/NTFL_1/The_2_Sigma_Effect.pdf

[4] Guskey, T. R. (2007/2008). The rest of the story. *Educational Leadership, 65*(4), 28–35.

[5] Carr, J. (2000). Technical issues of grading methods. In E. Trumbull & B. Farr (Eds.), *Grading and reporting student progress in an age of standards* (pp. 45–70). Norwood, MA: Christopher-Gordon.

[6] Brookhart, S. M. (2008). *How to give effective feedback to your students.* Alexandria, VA: Association for Supervision and Curriculum Development.

[7] National Research Council. (1996). *National science education standards.* Washington, DC: National Academies Press. Retrieved from http://www.nap.edu/catalog/4962.html. See p. 87.

[8] Rockow, M. (2008). This isn't English class! Using writing as an assessment tool in science. *Science Scope, 31*(5), 22–26.

[9] Sexton, U., & Solano-Flores, G. (2002, April). *Cultural validity in assessment: A cross-cultural study of the interpretation of mathematics and science test items.* Paper presented at the annual meeting of the American Educational Research Association, New Orleans.

[10] Wiggins, G., & McTighe, J. (1998). *Understanding by design.* Alexandria, VA: Association for Supervision and Curriculum Development.

[11] Darling-Hammond, L., & Richardson, N. (2009). Teacher learning: What matters? *Educational Leadership, 66*(5), 46–55; Loucks-Horsley, S., Love, N., Stiles, K. E., Mundry, S., & Hewson, P. W. (2003). *Designing professional development for teachers of science and mathematics.* Thousand Oaks, CA: Corwin Press.

CHAPTER 7

Putting It All Together

> **The art of simplicity is the puzzle of complexity.**
>
> — Doug Horton

In the prior chapters, we have described a framework for teaching diverse learners, the education-related characteristics of English learners and students with learning difficulties, strategies to build academic vocabulary and discourse, strategies to scaffold access to content addressing state standards, and strategies for fairly and accurately using classroom assessments. We discussed embedding strategies within the framework for teaching. Throughout, our singular focus has been on a very doable, yet highly effective approach for teaching and assessing all students in academic classes.

As conveyed earlier, we think two practices are particularly important for working with English learners and students with learning difficulties:

» Supporting concise *teacher talk with visuals*, especially graphic organizers, for students who need to see concepts and connections, and

» Providing plenty of opportunities for guided, meaningful *small-group work* that is often inquiry-based for students who need reinforcement, practice, social skills development, and an enjoyable classroom in which diversity is respected and appreciated. Pairs and trios ensure each group member has the opportunity to actively participate.

In this chapter, we provide a unit lesson plan template and describe how teachers can use it to create lesson plans that put into practice the ideas and strategies in this guidebook to provide effective support for all students, particularly English learners and students with learning difficulties.

TEMPLATE FOR PERSONALIZED LESSONS

This template for planning a unit lesson provides a checklist of the six scaffolding strategies within the framework of the 5 Es. A teacher writes how a strategy will be used — what the teacher will do and what the students will do individually or in small groups such as pairs, triads, or foursomes. Vocabulary building strategies and tools (see chapter 4) could be included. For a lesson with co-teaching, symbols might be used to indicate who does what, such as "G" for the general education teacher and "S" for the special education teacher or other specialist (e.g., ELD/ESL).

Following the blank lesson template is a sample plan for a day's lesson. Our intention is simply to apply vocabulary building strategies/tools (chapter 4), content scaffolding strategies (chapter 5), and classroom assessment strategies (chapter 6) to a contextualized lesson — it is not meant to be a model lesson in the sense of presenting everything a teacher might plan to do.

TEMPLATE FOR PLANNING PERSONALIZED LESSONS					
Grade:	Lesson:				
Content Objective(s):				Language Objective(s):	
		Scaffolding Strategies	What will I do? How will I personalize it?	What will students do? What will targeted students do?	**Evaluate** (check for understanding)
Engage	Teacher-Led	Cue – Advance Organizer Visuals K of KWL+ Think-Pair-Share			
Explore		Cue – Hints Think Aloud (model) Visuals W of KWL+ Think-Pair-Share Note Taking			
Explain	Student-Led, Teacher Guidance	Cue – Thinking Questions Think Aloud (apply) Visuals L of KWL+ Think-Pair-Share Summarizing/Inferring			
Elaborate		Cue – Hints/Questions Visuals Think-Pair-Share Summarizing Generalizing			
Reading/Other Materials					

SAMPLE PLAN FOR A DAY

Grade: 9	**Lesson: English** The unit is intended to teach students how use of language for imagery creates appeal to the senses of its audience. The lesson will examine classic literature, plays, and poems. This lesson targets allusions in Shakespeare's *Hamlet;* prior lessons targeted alliteration, foreshadowing, metaphor, and simile.

Content Objective: Students will identify and explain orally and in writing how Shakespeare used **allusions**, a type of figurative language and literary device, to create imagery in *Hamlet*.	**Language Objective**: Students will demonstrate their understanding of the word *allusion* by completing vocabulary journal templates (Frayer Model) and using the target word in structured academic talk.

		Scaffolding Strategies	What will I do? How will I personalize it?	What will students do? What will targeted students do?	**Evaluate** (check for understanding)
Engage	Teacher-Led	✓Cue – Advance Organizer ✓Visuals ✓K/W of KWL+ ✓Think-Pair-Share	**Advance Organizer:** Display Literary Devices **Graphic Organizer:** *Hamlet Prince of Denmark*, with prior lesson topics completed and the new topic, allusions, highlighted. Before starting allusions in *Hamlet*, display example allusion: "She was no <u>Sleeping Beauty</u>." Ask who has read this story. What does this allusion mean? **K of KWL chart:** What do you think an allusion is? Why do you think an author uses an allusion? **W of KWL chart:** What do you want to learn about allusions? Call on a few volunteers to share which words they recognize and from where or how they know them (e.g., Greek mythology, Ancient Rome, classic fairy tales); which words they don't know and how they can find the meaning/information.	**Think-Pair-Share:** 1 minute for trios to brainstorm the meaning of the allusion for Sleeping Beauty. **Think-Pair-Share:** personalized for some students who know Spanish or Mexican culture. Everyone says Mary is another <u>Mother Theresa</u>. Maria is another <u>Milagros</u>. Juan has the perseverance of <u>Don Quixote</u>. Practice with harder examples. Patience of <u>Job</u>. Vanity is the <u>Achilles'</u> heel of a talented actress.	**Thumbs Up/Down:** Do you know the story of Sleeping Beauty? Give synopsis as needed. Substitute easier examples from movies or TV as needed. Check that English learners know what "image" means. "To understand an author's allusion, what do you need to know?"

SAMPLE PLAN FOR A DAY (CONTINUED)				
Grade: 9		**Lesson: English** The unit is intended to teach students how use of language for imagery creates appeal to the senses of its audience. The lesson will examine classic literature, plays, and poems. This lesson targets allusions in Shakespeare's *Hamlet;* prior lessons targeted alliteration, foreshadowing, metaphor, and simile.		
Content Objective: Students will identify and explain orally and in writing how Shakespeare used **allusions,** a type of figurative language and literary device, to create imagery in *Hamlet.*			**Language Objective:** Students will demonstrate their understanding of the word *allusion* by completing vocabulary journal templates (Frayer Model) and using the target word in structured academic talk.	
		Scaffolding Strategies	What will I do? How will I personalize it?	What will students do? What will targeted students do?	**Evaluate** (check for understanding)
Explore	Student-Led, Teacher Guidance	✓**Cue – Hints** ✓**Think Aloud** (model) ✓**Visuals** ✓**Think-Pair-Share** ✓**Note Taking**	Display Frayer Model (**Visual**). Draw from **K** of **KWL** chart to informally define an allusion and write "An <u>allusion</u> is a <u>reference</u> to (mention of) <u>something</u> or <u>someone familiar</u>."	Students copy definition into their journals; chorally read definition.	Identify unknown words (especially for English learners) and write on **Word Wall** with known synonyms (e.g., reference).
			Explain that many allusions refer to historical locations or mythological figures. Display examples.	Trios complete Frayer Model. Opportunity for trios to add information in their journals.	Monitor trios, give feedback.
			Direct trios to complete the Frayer Model in their journals (two parts of an allusion; example, nonexample).		
			Give page, ask trios to find the allusion. Remind trios to use **Discussion Starters** posted on the wall.	Trios find the target allusion. **Think-Pair-Share:** "How was Polonius like Jephthah?"	[He also lost a daughter, Ophelia spying on Hamlet.]
			Identify and display the passage, highlight the allusion "O Jephthah, judge of Israel, what a treasure hadst thou!"		
			Model how to determine its meaning using **Think Aloud.**		
			Give worksheet with five pages in *Hamlet* (and modern-day version) that contain allusions.	Give target groups Sentence Frames for journal entries. Triads identify the allusion and determine its meaning and importance, then write answers in their journals, searching word sources as necessary.	Monitor group discussions and journal entries; give feedback, hints, cues as needed.
			Assign allusions/pages and direct triads to identify the allusions and determine their meaning.		

SAMPLE PLAN FOR A DAY (CONTINUED)

Grade: 9	**Lesson: English** The unit is intended to teach students how use of language for imagery creates appeal to the senses of its audience. The lesson will examine classic literature, plays, and poems. This lesson targets allusions in Shakespeare's *Hamlet;* prior lessons targeted alliteration, foreshadowing, metaphor, and simile.			
Content Objective: Students will identify and explain orally and in writing how Shakespeare used **allusions**, a type of figurative language and literary device, to create imagery in *Hamlet*.			**Language Objective:** Students will demonstrate their understanding of the word *allusion* by completing vocabulary journal templates (Frayer Model) and using the target word in structured academic talk.	
		Scaffolding Strategies	What will I do? How will I personalize it?	What will students do? What will targeted students do?	**Evaluate** (check for understanding)
Explain	**Student-Led, Teacher Guidance**	✓**Visuals** ✓**L of KWL+** ✓**Think-Pair-Share** ✓**Summarizing/ Inferring**	Select triads to share their allusions with the whole group. Enter information in **L of KWL+** chart. Enter key words/phrases in the displayed **graphic organizer** introduced at the *engage* stage. Explain the connection between prior lessons and this lesson about literary devices.	Group member explains an allusion, and rest of the students **summarize** information in their journals.	Monitor journal writing. Pass out a half-page Ticket Out at the end of class. "Allusions are _____ that authors use to _____. Using allusions can be important because _____."
Elaborate			No *elaboration* stage for this lesson.		
Reading Materials: *Hamlet Prince of Denmark* by William Shakespeare and alternative text written in modern English (http://www.willyson.com/hamlet/)					

Process for Creating a Lesson Plan for Personalized Instruction

Personalized instruction can also be called *differentiated* instruction, but here we prefer the term *personalized* to emphasize that all students are unique persons, not just labeled categories. The 5 Es framework and strategies presented in this book provide a basic level of personalization for diverse learners.

Here is a list of steps for creating a lesson plan to further personalize instruction.

1. **Lesson Topic.** Select a lesson topic you are very comfortable teaching, perhaps a lesson in which you have great expertise and many students have been successful. Now focus on strategies to help more students be successful. It will take time and practice to tailor strategies and include more intensive interventions so all students are successful.

2. **Day or Unit Lesson.** Decide whether this initial effort will be a plan for a one-day lesson or an entire unit. If you are experienced and comfortable with the approaches here, you may want to create a lesson plan that covers an entire unit, maintaining sparse notes for each day's lesson

within the unit. If you're a novice teacher, we suggest creating a lesson plan for an entire unit, and then a similar lesson plan for the first day of instruction.

Allow plenty of time the first day to model expectations for students during a Think-Pair-Share, and establish pairs or trios for the activity or explain the purpose and use of a specific graphic organizer. Allow yourself time to reflect and make mental or written notes — treat this as an experiment and, as good scientists would do, be sure to reflect on teaching practices and take notes on how students respond and what students say and do.

3. **How Many Strategies.** Select strategies from this guidebook, keeping in mind how one strategy can support another strategy, such as using a quick Think-Pair-Share as part of KWL+. It will take time and practice to integrate all of the strategies into a unit lesson. Keep in mind that a strategy you use should be used very often or daily, especially for many students with learning difficulties who benefit from routines, and provide an alert when something in that routine will be changed later in the day or next day.

4. **Topic/Objectives.** Enter the topic of the lesson and content and language objectives.

5. **Materials.** In the last row, state what reading materials will be used, including, perhaps, websites and other resource materials.

6. **Engage Stage.** Briefly, but concretely state what you will do followed by what the students will do, including the name of the strategies. In the left column, put a checkmark next to strategies you will use.

7. *Explore, Explain, Elaborate* **Stages.** Leverage strategies to extend or repeat across many of the 5 Es. For example, if you're teaching language arts, you might introduce a graphic organizer during the *engage* stage and write in just the story title and author. During the *explore* stage, you might then use Think-Pair-Share to get students to identify information about main characters, the plot, the resolution, and supporting details, entering this information succinctly into the graphic organizer. You would then fill in information about a theme of the story during the *explain* stage.

8. **Tailor for Individual Students.** Review the draft lesson plan. Are the needs and interests of all students being met? Are there specific interests for one or two students that could easily be included, perhaps as concrete examples or metaphors? If, for example, your lesson is on inertia and you remember that one student has a keen interest in cars, you may want to use cars as a concrete example during the *engage* stage.

9. **Review by a Colleague.** Ideally, have a coach or colleague review your lesson plan and discuss anything that might be missing or unclear.

10. **Collegial Advice and Support.** Now try out this lesson plan, getting feedback on what goes well and not so well, using what you learned to improve the next lesson. Ideally there is a person or support group (e.g., professional learning community or book study group) with whom to discuss ideas.

We recommend that teachers bear in mind that when an English learner does not comprehend, it is likely because there are too many words heard or read that are unknown or sentence complexity is too high and the English learner cannot even get the gist. When a student with a learning difficulty does not comprehend or follow directions, it is likely because the information needs to be chunked into small units with more wait time for the student to process or information needs to be paired with visual supports before it is lost from working memory. As Albert Einstein said, "Make it as simple as possible, but not more so." In other words, the challenge is not to dumb down vocabulary or content, just to be more concrete and break things down into simpler parts. The more that visuals support oral or written language, the more likely an English learner or student with a learning difficulty will have the scaffolding to process new information at the level of native English speakers with no learning difficulties. The expert teachers find out how a student learns best, then teach the student by that approach.

Lastly, it is important to bear in mind that scaffolds are intended to be temporary — for instance, visual scaffolds can help to make content accessible for the student with a receptive processing difficulty, but if a specialist works with the student to strengthen listening skills over time, then eventually the scaffolding becomes less necessary and should be removed. A teacher might start using a new scaffolding strategy such as a graphic organizer by explaining its purpose and use, modeling it, and guiding students to use it (e.g., filling in the graphic organizer's boxes, bubbles, lines). Over time the teacher should shift responsibility to students, who individually or in small groups, select a graphic organizer appropriate for a given context. Once a student can write sentences, paragraphs, or longer discourse, the teacher should stop giving the student Sentence Frames and templates as writing scaffolds, but it is likely that the student will continue using a traditional outline format or graphic organizer to organize ideas before starting to write organized, connected, coherent text. This is teaching students to become lifelong learners and transition to postsecondary education and careers, where instructors and bosses may not provide such scaffolds.

CASE SCENARIO: DYLAN

Dylan is an eighth grade student with a diagnosis of Asperger syndrome. He participates full time in general education classes and receives weekly occupational therapy to improve his fine motor skills (e.g., handwriting). Once per month his general education teachers meet with his case manager, the special education teacher, to review his progress toward IEP goals. Dylan's mathematics teacher noticed that Dylan often has difficulty completing assignments, insisting on starting his work over if it does not "look right" (e.g., misalignment of numbers) and has ripped up his work on several occasions. Dylan prefers to solve problems mentally without writing down his work. Although Dylan has no difficulty remembering formulas, he has difficulty sequencing operational procedures to solve problems. Dylan's social studies and English teachers shared that his reading is fast, fluent, and accurate and that he has good comprehension of informational text. They stated that although his receptive and expressive vocabularies are below age level, he could master concepts that are supported with visuals. All of his teachers noted that when they gave only oral instruction, Dylan tended to look disinterested and, when questioned, did not fully understand the concepts taught.

Dylan's teachers decided to always support their oral instruction with visuals for Dylan and students with similar auditory learning weaknesses. Also, they decided that Dylan could use a laptop or graphic organizers to take notes while his hand coordination was developing. His math teacher collaborated with the special education teacher to design worksheets with vertical lines and provided a clear ruler to help Dylan align numbers when doing computations.

CASE SCENARIO: JESSE

Mr. Gonzales, an educator for more than a decade who teaches upper middle grade science, expressed concern about one of his students, Jesse. Mr. Gonzales described Jesse as having difficulty listening, organizing, and following through with work, demonstrating easy distractibility and impulsive behaviors during his science class, especially when asked to produce lengthy written work or engage in group learning activities. Mr. Gonzales consulted with colleagues who also taught Jesse and discovered that he was exhibiting similar behaviors in their classes. They reported that Jesse frequently gets out of his seat during class, interrupts his peers, and often talks back when corrected. Samples of his written work showed illegible handwriting, poor command of the conventions of standard English, and difficulty communicating experiences or information in written format. He had missing and late assignments. Mr. Gonzales noted that his school record showed a recommendation from the student study team to seek medical advice for a possible formal diagnosis for ADHD.

Mr. Gonzales decided he would use instructional strategies targeted to help Jesse's difficulties in social exchanges and in the areas of written expression. Mr. Gonzales decided he needed to model the social skills expected in his classroom during group work, using Think Aloud for Jesse and other students with similar social skills needs. He strategically assigned students to work in pairs or triads, making certain that students with learning difficulties were grouped with students without identified disabilities. He placed groups in the room so as to reduce potential conflicts resulting from placing students with poor impulse control or emotional control in the same vicinity. He built in cues of the task to be done or the behavior to be performed and posted Discussion Starters (see chapter 4). He explicitly taught, practiced, reinforced, and retaught certain social skills as needed. He started using Think-Pair-Share with very brief time spans for students to interact in the pair/triad and gradually increased task time as Jesse and targeted students became more adept. It was normal in his class to start with brief small-group task time and shift to extended time for deeper critical thinking and meaningful tasks.

Mr. Gonzales used graphic organizers for recording and recalling information, specifically addressing the goal of the lesson or unit development, such as a cause and effect sequential graph to demonstrate the effects of global warming. The organizer was then used as an outline to complete written assignments and to guide whole- and small-group discussion relating to the topic of study. In addition, Mr. Gonzales developed and taught the class how to use a rubric designed to develop and strengthen writing through self-evaluating the quality of written work. The rubric addressed the attributes of the development of writing, such as ideas and content, word choice, sentence fluency, organization, voice, and proofreading.

References

Abedi, J. (2002, Spring). Assessment and accommodations of English language learners: Issues, concerns, and recommendations. *Journal of School Improvement, 3*(1). Retrieved from http://www.icsac.org/jsi/2002v3i1/assessment

Albus, D., Thurlow, M., & Clapper, A. (2007). *Standards-based instructional strategies for English language learners with disabilities* (ELLs with Disabilities Report 18). Minneapolis: University of Minnesota, National Center on Educational Outcomes.

Alexander, P. A., Kulikowich, J. M., & Schulze, S. K. (1994). How subject-matter knowledge affects recall and interest. *American Educational Research Journal, 31*(2), 313–337.

American Psychiatric Association. (2000). *Diagnostic and statistical manual of mental disorders* (4th ed., text rev.). Washington, DC: Author.

Anderson, L. W., & Krathwohl, D. R. (Eds.). (2001). *A taxonomy for learning, teaching and assessing: A revision of Bloom's Taxonomy of educational objectives*. New York: Longman.

Anderson-Inman, L., Knox-Quinn, C., & Horney, M. A. (1996). Computer-based study strategies for students with learning disabilities: Individual differences associated with adoption level. *Journal of Learning Disabilities, 29*(5), 461–484.

Anstrom, K. (1999). *Preparing secondary education teachers to work with English language learners: Mathematics* (NCBE Resource Collection Series, No. 14). Washington, DC: National Clearinghouse for Bilingual Education.

August, D., & Shanahan, T. (2010). Effective literacy instruction for English learners. In California Department of Education (Ed.), *Improving education for English learners: Research-based approaches* (pp. 209–250). Sacramento: California Department of Education.

Baker, P. H., Murray, M., Murray-Slutsky, C., & Paris, B. (2010). Faces of autism. *Educational Leadership, 68*(2), 40–45.

Barkley, R. A. (1997). *ADHD and the nature of self-control*. New York: Guilford Press.

Barrera, M., Liu, K., Thurlow, M., Shyyan, V., Yan, M., & Chamberlain, S. (2006). *Math strategy instruction for students with disabilities who are learning English* (ELLs with Disabilities Report 15). Minneapolis: University of Minnesota, National Center on Educational Outcomes.

Bashe, P. R., & Kirby, B. L. (2005). *The OASIS guide to Asperger syndrome: Advice, support, insight, and inspiration*. New York: Crowne Publishing.

Bay-Williams, J. M., & Herrera, S. (2007). Is "just good teaching" enough to support the learning of English language learners? Insights from sociocultural learning theory. In W. G. Martin, M. E. Strutchens, & P. C. Elliott (Eds.), *The learning of mathematics: Sixty-ninth yearbook* (pp. 43–63). Reston, VA: National Council of Teachers of Mathematics.

Beck, I. L., McKeown, M. G., & Kucan, L. (2002). *Bringing words to life: Robust vocabulary instruction.* New York: Guilford Press.

Bender, W. (2008a). *Differentiating instruction for students with learning disabilities.* Thousand Oaks, CA: Corwin Press.

Bender, W. (2008b). *Learning disabilities: Characteristics, identification, and teaching strategies.* Columbus, OH: Merrill.

Bereiter, C., & Bird, M. (1985). Use of thinking aloud in identification and teaching of reading comprehension strategies. *Cognition and Instruction, 2,* 131–156.

Bergeson, T., Davidson, C., Harmon, B., Gill, D. H., & Colwell, M. L. (2008). *The educational aspects of autism spectrum disorders.* Olympia, WA: Special Education, Office of Superintendent of Public Instruction. Retrieved from www.k12.wa.us/SpecialEd/pubdocs/Autism%20Manual.pdf

Black, P., & William, D. (1998). Inside the black box: Raising standards through classroom assessment. *Phi Delta Kappan, 80*(2), 139–149. Retrieved from http://www.pdkintl.org/kappan/kbla9810.htm

Bloom, B. (1984). The 2 sigma problem: The search for methods of group instruction as effective as one-to-one tutoring. *Educational Researcher, 13*(6), 4–16. Retrieved from http://dlsystems.us/readings/NTFL_1/The_2_Sigma_Effect.pdf

Boaler, J., & Humphreys, C. (2005). *Connecting mathematical ideas: Middle school video cases to support teaching and learning.* Portsmouth, NH: Heinemann.

Boyle, J. R., & Weishaar, M. (1997). The effects of expert-generated versus student-generated cognitive organizers on the reading comprehension of students with learning disabilities. *Learning Disabilities Research & Practice, 12*(4), 228–235.

Bremer, C. D., Vaughn, S., Clapper, A. T., & Kim, A-H. (2002). Collaborative strategic reading (CSR): Improving secondary students' reading comprehension skills. *NCSET Research to Practice Brief, 1*(2). Retrieved from http://www.ncset.org/publications/viewdesc.asp?id=424

Brookbank, D., Grover, S., Kullberg, K., & Strawser, C. (1999). *Improving student achievement through organization of student learning.* Chicago: Master's Action Research Project, Saint Xavier University and IRI/Skylight. (ERIC Document Reproduction Service No. ED435094)

Brookhart, S. M. (2008). *How to give effective feedback to your students.* Alexandria, VA: Association for Supervision and Curriculum Development.

Buchanan, K., & Helman, M. (1997). *Reforming mathematics instruction for ESL literacy students.* Washington, DC: ERIC Clearinghouse on Languages and Linguistics.

Buffum, A., Mattos, M., & Weber, C. (2010). The why behind RTI. *Educational Leadership, 68*(2), 10–17.

Bulgren, J., Schumaker, J. B., & Deschler, D. D. (1988). Effectiveness of a concept teaching routine in enhancing the performance of LD students in secondary-level mainstream classes. *Learning Disability Quarterly, 11*(1), 3–17.

Burnett, G. E. (2010, October 27). Erasing the special-ed stigma: Students given chance in mainstream classes. *The Dispatch.* Retrieved from http://www.cdispatch.com

Bybee, R. W. (1997). *Achieving scientific literacy: From purposes to practices.* Portsmouth, NH: Heinemann.

California Department of Education. (2000). *Strategic teaching and learning: Standards-based instruction to promote content literacy in grades four through twelve.* Sacramento: California Department of Education Press.

California Department of Education. (2010). *Improving education for English learners: Research-based approaches.* Sacramento: California Department of Education.

Cambell, A. E., Adams, V. M., & Davis, G. E. (2007). Cognitive demands and second-language learners: A framework for analyzing mathematics instructional contexts. *Mathematical Thinking and Learning, 9*(1), 3–30.

Carolan, J., & Guinn, A. (2007). Differentiation: Lessons from master teachers. *Educational Leadership, 64*(5), 44–47.

Carr, J. (2000). Technical issues of grading methods. In E. Trumbull & B. Farr (Eds.), *Grading and reporting student progress in an age of standards* (pp. 45–70). Norwood, MA: Christopher-Gordon.

Carr, J., Carroll, C., Cremer, S., Gale, M., Lagunoff, R., & Sexton, U. (2009). *Making mathematics accessible to English learners: A guidebook for teachers.* San Francisco: WestEd.

Carr, J., Sexton, U., & Lagunoff, R. (2007). *Making science accessible to English learners: A guidebook for teachers.* San Francisco: WestEd.

Cassidy, S., Ramirez, D., Bakken, C., Gadzuk, N., & Alvarez-Martini, M. (2011). Students enrolled in California public schools diagnosed with autism. *The Multilingual Educator,* 34–38. Retrieved from http://wexford.org/wexford_files_files/CABE%20Autism%20Article.pdf

Chamot, A. U., & O'Malley, J. M. (1994). *The Calla handbook: Implementing the Cognitive Academic Language Learning Approach.* White Plains, NY: Addison Wesley Longman.

Chapin, S., & O'Connor, C. (2007). Academically productive talk: Supporting students' learning in mathematics. In W. G. Martin, M. E. Strutchens, & P. C. Elliott (Eds.), *The learning of mathematics: Sixty-ninth yearbook* (pp. 113–128). Reston, VA: National Council of Teachers of Mathematics.

Chappuis, S., & Chappuis, J. (2007/2008). The best value in formative assessment. *Educational Leadership, 65*(4), 14–19.

Clegg, J. (Ed.). (1996). *Mainstreaming ESL: Case studies in integrating ESL students into the mainstream curriculum.* Clevedon, UK: Multilingual Matters.

Coggins, D., Kravin, D., Coates, G. D., & Carroll, M. D. (2007). *English language learners in the mathematics classroom.* Thousand Oaks, CA: Corwin Press.

Cohen, E. G. (1994). *Designing groupwork: Strategies for the heterogeneous classroom.* New York: Teachers College Press.

Cole, R. W. (Ed.). (1995). *Educating everybody's children: Diverse teaching strategies for diverse learners.* Alexandria, VA: Association for Supervision and Curriculum Development.

Cole, R. W. (Ed.). (2001). *More strategies for educating everybody's children.* Alexandria, VA: Association for Supervision and Curriculum Development.

Common Core State Standards Initiative. (2010). *English language arts standards.* Retrieved from http://www.corestandards.org/the-standards/english-language-arts-standards

Cummins, J., & Swain, M. (1986). *Bilingualism in education: Aspects of theory, research and practice.* London: Longman.

Curwin, R. L., Mendler, A. N., & Mendler, B. D. (2008). *Discipline with dignity* (3rd ed.). Alexandria, VA: Association for Supervision and Curriculum Development.

Darling-Hammond, L., & Richardson, N. (2009). Teacher learning: What matters? *Educational Leadership, 66*(5), 46–55.

Dawson, P., & Guare, R. (2010). *Executive skills in children and adolescents: A practical guide to assessment and intervention.* New York: Guilford Press.

DeRuvo, S. L. (2009). *Strategies for teaching adolescents with ADHD.* San Francisco: Jossey-Bass.

Diaz-Rico, L., & Weed, K. (2002). *The crosscultural language and academic development handbook* (2nd ed.). Needham Heights, MA: Allyn & Bacon.

DiCecco, V. M., & Gleason, M. M. (2002). Using graphic organizers to attain relational knowledge from expository text. *Journal of Learning Disabilities, 35*(4), 306–320.

Dornan, R., Rosen, L. M., & Wilson, M. (2005). Lesson designs for reading comprehension and vocabulary development. In P. A. Richard-Amato & M. A. Snow (Eds.), *Academic success for English language learners* (pp. 248–274). White Plains, NY: Pearson Education.

Duran, E., Duran, L., Haney, J., & Scheuermann, A. (2011, March). A learning cycle for all students. *The Science Teacher, 78*(3), 56–60.

Dutro, S., & Moran, C. (2003). Rethinking English language instruction: An architectural approach. In G. G. Garcia (Ed.), *English learners: Reaching the highest level of English literacy* (pp. 227–258). Newark, DE: International Reading Association.

Echevarría, J., Vogt, M., & Short, D. J. (2008). *Making content comprehensible for English learners: The SIOP© model* (3rd ed.). Boston: Allyn & Bacon.

Echevarría, J., Vogt, M., & Short, D. J. (2010). *Making content comprehensible for secondary English language learners.* Boston, MA: Allyn & Bacon.

The Educator's PLN. http://edupln.ning.com

Ellerton, N. F., & Clarkson, P. C. (1996). Language factors in mathematics teaching and learning. In A. J. Bishop, K. Clements, C. Keitel, J. Kilpatrick, & C. Laborde (Eds.), *International handbook of mathematics education* (pp. 987–1033). Dordrecht, Netherlands: Kluwer.

Ellis, E. S., & Worthington, L. A. (2004). *Research synthesis on effective teaching principles and the design of quality tools for educators.* Eugene, OR: National Center to Improve the Tools of Educators, University of Oregon. Retrieved from http://www.iu17.org/393999727151823/lib/393999727151823/Effective%20 Teaching.pdf

Ellis, R. (2003). *Task-based language learning and teaching.* Cary, NC: Oxford Applied Linguistics.

Fathman, A. K., Quinn, M. E., & Kessler, C. (1992). *Teaching science to English learners, grades 4–8* (NCBE Program Information Guide Series No. 11). Washington, DC: National Clearinghouse for Bilingual Education. Retrieved from http://www.ncela.gwu.edu/files/rcd/BE018764/PIG11.pdf

Fillmore, L. W. (1976). *The second time around: Cognitive and social strategies in second language acquisition* (Unpublished doctoral dissertation). Stanford University, Stanford, CA.

Fisher, D., & Frey, N. (2007). *Checking for understanding: Formative assessment techniques for your classroom.* Alexandria, VA: Association for Supervision and Curriculum Development.

Fisher, D., Roach, V., & Frey, N. (2002). Examining the general programmatic benefits of inclusive schools. *International Journal of Inclusive Education, 6*(1), 63–78.

Flynn, K., & Hill, J. (2005). *English language learners: A growing population* (McREL Policy Brief). Denver, CO: Mid-continent Research for Education and Learning. Retrieved from http://www.mcrel.org/pdf/policybriefs/5052pi_pbenglishlanguagelearners.pdf

Frayer, D., Frederick, W. C., & Klausmeier, H. J. (1969). *A schema for testing the level of cognitive mastery.* Madison: Wisconsin Center for Education Research. A brief description can be retrieved from http://www.justreadnow.com/strategies/frayer.htm

Freeman, D. J. (2004). Teaching in the context of English-language learners: What we need to know. In M. Sadowski (Ed.), *Teaching immigrant and second-language students: Strategies for success* (pp. 7-20). Cambridge, MA: Harvard Education Press.

Freeman, D., & Freeman, Y. (1988). *Sheltered English instruction* (ERIC Digest, ED301070). Washington, DC: ERIC Clearinghouse on Languages and Linguistics. Retrieved from http://www.ericdigests.org/pre-9210/english.htm

Frey, N., Fisher, D., & Everlove, S. (2009). *Productive group work: How to engage students, build teamwork, and promote understanding.* Alexandria, VA: Association for Supervision and Curriculum Development.

Friend, M., & Bursuck, W. (2002). *Including students with special needs: A practical guide for classroom teachers.* Needham Heights, MA: Allyn & Bacon.

Garner, B. K. (2007). *Getting to "got it!" Helping struggling students learn how to learn.* Alexandria, VA: Association for Supervision and Curriculum Development.

Gersten, R., Baker, S. K., & Marks, S. U. (1998). *Teaching English-language learners with learning difficulties: Guiding principles and examples from research-based practice* (ERIC Publications ED427448). Retrieved from http://www.eric.ed.gov/ERICWebPortal/detail?accno=ED427448

Gersten, R., Compton, D., Connor, C. M., Dimino, J., Santoro, L., Linan-Thompson, S., & Tilly, W. D. (2008). *Assisting students struggling with reading: Response to Intervention and multi-tier intervention for reading in the primary grades. A practice guide* (NCEE 2009-4045). Washington, DC: National Center for Education Evaluation and Regional Assistance, Institute of Education Sciences, U.S. Department of Education. Retrieved from http://ies.ed.gov/ncee/wwc/publications/practiceguides/

Gibbons, P. (2002). *Scaffolding language, scaffolding learning: Teaching second language learners in the mainstream classroom.* Portsmouth, NH: Heinemann.

Grandin, T. (1986). *Emergence: Labeled autistic.* New York: Grand Central Publishing.

Grandin, T. (1995). *Thinking in pictures: My life with autism.* New York: Vintage Books.

Grandin, T. (2007). Autism from the inside. *Educational Leadership, 64*(5), 29-33.

Gregory, G., & Chapman, C. (2001). *Differentiated instructional strategies: One size doesn't fit all.* Thousand Oaks, CA: Corwin Press.

Guskey, T. R. (2000). *Evaluating professional development.* Thousand Oaks, CA: Corwin Press.

Guskey, T. R. (2007/2008). The rest of the story. *Educational Leadership, 65*(4), 28-35.

Gutierres, M. (2010, August 16). Sac City, Elk Grove follow trend of bringing special-ed students back to neighborhood schools. *The Sacramento Bee.* Retrieved from http://www.sacbee.com

Hall, T., & Strangman, N. (2002). *Graphic organizers.* Wakefield, MA: National Center on Accessing the General Curriculum. Retrieved from http://aim.cast.org/learn/historyarchive/backgroundpapers/graphic_organizers

Harlev, R. (2005). Contented learning. *Language, 4*(9), 22–27.

Hawken, L. S., Vincent, C. G., & Schumann, J. (2008). Response to intervention for social behavior: Challenges and opportunities. *Journal of Emotional and Behavioral Disorders, 16*(4), 213–225.

Hawkins, B. (2005). Mathematics education for second language students in the mainstream classroom. In P. A. Richard-Amato & M. A. Snow (Eds.), *Academic success for English language learners* (pp. 337–397). White Plains, NY: Pearson Education.

Hayden, D., & Cuevas, G. (1990). *Pre-algebra lexicon.* Washington, DC: Center for Applied Linguistics.

Heller, R., & Greenleaf, C. (2007). *Literacy instruction in the content areas: Getting to the core of middle and high school improvement.* Washington, DC: Alliance for Excellent Education.

Herrell, A. L., & Jordan, M. L. (2003). *Fifty strategies for teaching English language learners.* Englewood Cliffs, NJ: Prentice Hall.

Hill, J. D., & Flynn, K. M. (2006). *Classroom instruction that works for English language learners.* Alexandria, VA: Association for Supervision and Curriculum Development.

Huber, C. (2010). Professional learning 2.0. *Educational Leadership, 67*(8), 41–46.

Hudson, P., Lignugaris-Kraft, B., & Miller, T. (1993). Using content enhancements to improve the performance of adolescents with learning disabilities in content classes. *Learning Disabilities Research & Practice, 8*(2), 106–126.

Hyerle, D. (1996). *Visual tools for constructing knowledge.* Alexandria, VA: Association for Supervision and Curriculum Development.

Institute for the Advancement of Research in Education (IARE) at AEL. (2003). *Graphic organizers: A review of scientifically based research.* Portland, OR: Inspiration Software.

Jarrett, D. (1999a). *The inclusive classroom: Teaching mathematics and science for students with learning disabilities. It's just good teaching.* Portland, OR: Northwest Regional Educational Laboratory.

Jarrett, D. (1999b). *The inclusive classroom: Teaching mathematics and science to English-language learners. It's just good teaching.* Portland, OR: Northwest Regional Educational Laboratory.

Kang, H., & Pham, K. T. (1995, March). *From 1 to Z: Integrating math and language learning* (ERIC Document Reproduction Service No. ED 381 031). Paper presented at the 29th annual meeting of Teachers of English to Speakers of Other Languages, Long Beach, CA.

Khisty, L. L., & Chval, K. B. (2002). Pedagogic discourse and equity in mathematics: When teachers' talk matters. *Mathematics Education Research Journal, 14*(3), 4–18.

Kim, A., Vaughn, S., Wanzek, J., & Wei, S. (2004). Graphic organizers and their effects on the reading comprehension of students with LD: A synthesis of research. *Journal of Learning Disabilities, 37*(2), 105–118. For a summary, see http://nichcy.org/research/summaries/abstract21

Kinsella, K. (2007). *Language strategies for active classroom participation.* San Francisco: San Francisco State University. Retrieved as a document named LanguageClassDiscussion.doc from http://www.sccoe.org/depts/ell/kinsella.asp

Krashen, S. D. (1981). *Second language acquisition and second language learning.* New York: Pergamon.

Krashen, S. D. (1985). *The input hypothesis: Issues and implications.* New York: Longman.

Laborde, C. (1990). Language and mathematics. In P. Nesher & J. Kilpatrick (Eds.), *Mathematics and cognition: A research synthesis by the International Group for the Psychology of Mathematics Education* (pp. 53–69). Cambridge: Cambridge University Press.

Lehr, F., Osborn, J., & Hiebert, E. H. (2005). *A focus on vocabulary* [second in the Research-Based Practices in Early Reading Series]. Honolulu, HI: Regional Educational Laboratory at Pacific Resources for Education and Learning. Retrieved from http://www.prel.org/products/re_/ES0419.htm

Levenson, N. (2011). *Something has got to change: Rethinking special education*. Washington, DC: American Enterprise Institute for Public Policy Research. Retrieved from http://www.aei.org/papers/education/something-has-got-to-change-rethinking-special-education

Long, M. H. (1981). Input, interaction, and second language acquisition. *Annals of the New York Academy of Science, 379,* 259–278.

Loucks-Horsley, S., Love, N., Stiles, K. E., Mundry, S., & Hewson, P. W. (2003). *Designing professional development for teachers of science and mathematics*. Thousand Oaks, CA: Corwin Press.

Lougy, R., DeRuvo, S., & Rosenthal, D. (2007). *Teaching young children with ADHD: Successful strategies and practical interventions for preK–3*. Thousand Oaks, CA: Corwin Press.

Lovitt, T., Rudsit, J., Jenkins, J., Pious, C., & Benedetti, D. (1985). Two methods of adapting science materials for learning disabled and regular seventh graders. *Learning Disability Quarterly, 8,* 275–285.

Lyman, F. (1992). Think-pair-share, thinktrix, thinklinks, and weird facts. In N. Davidson & T. Worsham (Eds.), *Enhancing thinking through cooperative learning* (pp. 169–181). New York: Teachers College Press.

Martin, T. S. (Ed.). (2007). *Mathematics teaching today* (2nd ed.). Reston, VA: National Council of Teachers of Mathematics.

Marzano, R. J. (2000). *Transforming classroom grading*. Arlington, VA: Association for Supervision and Curriculum Development.

Marzano, R. J., & Pickering, D. J. (2005). *Building academic vocabulary: Teacher's manual*. Alexandria, VA: Association for Supervision and Curriculum Development.

Marzano, R. J., Pickering, D. J., & Pollock, J. E. (2001). *Classroom instruction that works: Research-based strategies for increasing student achievement*. Alexandria, VA: Association for Supervision and Curriculum Development.

Mason, J., Burton, L., & Stacey, K. (1982). *Thinking mathematically*. London: Addison-Wesley.

Mastropieri, M. A., & Scruggs, T. E. (1998). Enhancing school success with mnemonic strategies. *Intervention in School and Clinic, 33*(4), 201–208.

McCall-Perez, Z. (2005). *Grouping English learners for science*. Unpublished manuscript.

Mestre, J. (1988). The role of language comprehension in mathematics and problem solving. In R. Cocking & J. Mestre (Eds.), *Linguistic and cultural influences on learning mathematics* (pp. 201–220). Hillsdale, NJ: Lawrence Erlbaum.

Monroe, E. E., & Panchyshyn, R. (1995). Vocabulary considerations for teaching mathematics. *Childhood Education, 72*(2), 80–83.

Moore, D. W., & Readence, J. E. (1984). A quantitative and qualitative review of graphic organizer research. *Journal of Educational Research, 78*(1), 11–17.

Moschkovich, J. (1999). Supporting the participation of English language learners in mathematical discussions. *For the Learning of Mathematics, 19*(1), 11–19.

Narkon, D. E., Wells, J. C., & Segal, L. S. (2011, March/April). E-word wall: An interactive vocabulary instruction tool for students with learning disabilities and autism spectrum disorders. *Teaching Exceptional Children, 43*(4), 38–47.

National Center on Response to Intervention. (n.d.). *The essential components of RTI.* Retrieved from http://www.rti4success.org/whatisrti

National Clearinghouse on Bilingual Education. (1987). Sheltered English: An approach to content area instruction for limited-English-proficient students. *Forum, 10*(6), 1–3.

National Commission on Teaching and America's Future. (2011). Team up for 21st century teaching and learning. *ASCD Express, 6*(19). Retrieved from http://www.ascd.org/ascdexpress

National Council of Teachers of Mathematics. (2000). *Principles and standards for school mathematics.* Reston, VA: Author.

National Professional Development Center on Autism Spectrum Disorders. (2008a). Session 1: Understanding pervasive developmental disorders and autism spectrum disorder. In *Foundations of autism spectrum disorders: An online course.* Chapel Hill, NC: FPG Child Development Institute, University of North Carolina.

National Professional Development Center on Autism Spectrum Disorders. (2008b). Session 2: Characteristics of learners with autism spectrum disorders. In *Foundations of autism spectrum disorders: An online course.* Chapel Hill: FPG Child Development Institute, University of North Carolina.

National Reading Panel. (2000). *Teaching children to read: An evidence-based assessment of the scientific research literature on reading and its implications for reading instruction* (NIH Pub. No. 00-4769). Washington, DC: U.S. Department of Health and Human Services, National Institutes of Health.

National Research Council. (1996). *National science education standards.* Washington, DC: National Academies Press. Retrieved from http://www.nap.edu/catalog/4962.html

National Research Council. (1999). *How people learn: Bridging research and practice.* Washington, DC: National Academies Press.

National Research Council. (2005). *How students learn: History, mathematics, and science in the classroom.* Washington, DC: National Academies Press.

Nowacek, E. J., & Mamlin, N. (2007, Spring). General education teachers and students with ADHD: What modifications are made? *Preventing School Failure, 51*(3), 28.

Ozonoff, S., & Griffith, E. M. (2000). Neuropsychological function and the external validity of Asperger syndrome. In A. Klin, F. R. Volkmar, & S. S. Sparrow (Eds.), *Asperger syndrome* (pp. 72–96). New York: Guildford Press.

Padron, Y. N. (1993). Teaching and learning risks associated with limited cognitive mastery in science and mathematics for limited English proficient students. In *Proceedings of the third national research symposium on LEP student issues: Focus on middle and high school issues* (Vol. II). Washington, DC: U.S. Department of Education, Office of Bilingual Education and Minority Languages Affairs.

Pittman, G. (2011, August 23). Writing problems common in kids with ADHD. ABS-CBNNews.com. Retrieved from http://www.abs-cbnnews.com/lifestyle/08/23/11/writing-problems-common-kids-adhd

Pressley, M., & Afflerbach, P. (1995). *Verbal protocols of reading: The nature of constructively responsive reading.* Hillsdale, NJ: Lawrence Erlbaum.

Rea, P. J., McLaughlin, V. L., & Walther-Thomas, C. (2002). Outcomes for students with learning disabilities in inclusive and pullout programs. *Council for Exceptional Children, 68*(2), 203-223.

Rivera, M. O., Moughamian, A. C., Lesaux, N. K., & Francis, D. J. (2009). *Language and reading interventions for English language learners and English language learners with disabilities.* Portsmouth, NH: RMC Research Corporation, Center on Instruction. Retrieved from http://www.centeroninstruction.org/files/Lang%20 and%20Rdng%20Interventions%20for%20ELLs%20and%20ELLs%20with%20Disabilities.pdf

Rockow, M. (2008). This isn't English class! Using writing as an assessment tool in science. *Science Scope, 31*(5), 22-26.

Rosenberg, M. S., Westling, D. L., & McLeskey, J. (2008). *Special education for today's teachers: An introduction.* Columbus, OH: Merrill.

RTI Action Network. (n.d.). *What is RTI?* Retrieved from http://www.rtinetwork.org/learn/what/whatisrti

Scanlon, D., Deshler, D. D., & Schumaker, J. B. (1996). Can a strategy be taught and learned in secondary inclusive classrooms? *Learning Disabilities Research & Practice, 11*(1), 41-57.

Schetter, P. (2004). *Learning the R.O.P.E.S. for improved executive function: A cognitive behavioral approach for individuals with high functioning autism and other behavioral disorders.* Redding, CA: ABTA.

Schoenbach, R., Greenleaf, C. L., Cziko, C., & Hurwitz, L. (1999). *Reading for understanding: A guide to improving reading in middle and high school classrooms.* San Francisco: Jossey-Bass.

Scruggs, T. E., Mastropieri, M. A., Berkeley, S., & Graetz, J. E. (2009). Do special education interventions improve learning of secondary content? A meta-analysis. *Remedial & Special Education, 31*(6), 437-449. A summary can be retrieved from http://nichcy.org/research/summaries/abstract80

Sexton, U., & Solano-Flores, G. (2002, April). *Cultural validity in assessment: A cross-cultural study of the interpretation of mathematics and science test items.* Paper presented at the annual meeting of the American Educational Research Association, New Orleans.

Sherris, A. (2008, September). Integrated content and language instruction. In *CALdigest.* Washington, DC: Center for Applied Linguistics. Retrieved from http://www.cal.org

Short, D. (1993). Assessing integrating language and content. *TESOL Quarterly, 27*(4), 627-656.

Short, D. J., & Fitzsimmons, S. (2007). *Double the work: Challenges and solutions to acquiring language and academic literacy for adolescent English language learners.* New York: Alliance for Excellent Education.

Silver, H. F., Strong, R. W., & Perini, M. J. (2000). *So each may learn.* Alexandria, VA: Association for Supervision and Curriculum Development.

Silverman, L. K. (2002). *Upside-down brilliance: The visual-spatial learner.* Denver: DeLeon Publishing.

Slavin, R. E. (1995, October). *Research on cooperative learning and achievement: What we know, what we need to know* (No. OERI-R-117-D40005). Washington, DC: U.S. Dept. of Education. Retrieved from http:// socialfamily535.pbworks.com/f/slavin1996%5B1%5D.pdf

Sousa, D. A. (2001a). *How the brain learns: A classroom teacher's guide* (2nd ed.). Thousand Oaks, CA: Corwin Press.

Sousa, D. A. (2001b). *How the special needs brain learns.* Thousand Oaks, CA: Corwin Press.

Stahl, S. A., & Fairbanks, M. M. (1986). The effects of vocabulary instruction: A model-based meta-analysis. *Review of Educational Research, 56*(1), 72–110.

Steele, M. (2010, Summer). High school students with learning disabilities: Mathematics instruction, study skills, and high stakes tests. *American Secondary Education, 38*(3), 21–27.

Swales, J. M. (2005). Academically speaking. *Language Magazine, 4*(8), 30–34.

Teachers of English to Speakers of Other Languages (TESOL). PreK–12 English language proficiency standards framework. Retrieved from http://www.tesol.org/s_tesol/sec_document.asp?CID=281&DID=13323

Thurlow, M., Syyan, V., Barrera, M., & Liu, K. (2008). *Delphi study of instructional strategies for English language learners with disabilities: Recommendations from educators nationwide* (ELLs with Disabilities Report 21). Minneapolis: University of Minnesota, National Center on Educational Outcomes.

Tomlinson, C. A. (1999). *The differentiated classroom: Responding to the needs of all students.* Alexandria, VA: Association for Supervision and Curriculum Development.

Tomlinson, C. A., & Imbeau, M. B. (2010). *Leading and managing a differentiated classroom.* Alexandria, VA: Association for Supervision and Curriculum Development.

Tomlinson, C. A., & McTighe, J. (2006). *Integrating and differentiating instruction: Understanding by design.* Alexandria, VA: Association for Supervision and Curriculum Development.

Trumbull, E. (2000). Why do we grade — and should we? In E. Trumbull & B. Farr (Eds.), *Grading and reporting student progress in an age of standards* (pp. 23–44). Norwood, MA: Christopher-Gordon.

Trumbull, E., & Farr, B. (2005). *Language and learning: What teachers need to know.* Norwood, MA: Christopher-Gordon.

Vang, C. (2004). Teaching science to English learners. *Language Magazine, 4*(4).

Vaughn, B., & Kratochvil, C. (2006). Pharmacotherapy of ADHD in young children. *Psychiatry, 3*(8), 36–45.

Vygotsky, L. (1962). *Thought and language.* Cambridge, MA: MIT Press.

Vygotsky, L. (1986). *Thought and language* (A. Kozulin, Ed. and Trans.). Cambridge, MA: Harvard University Press.

Wagner, S. (2002). *Inclusive programming for middle school students with autism/Asperger's syndrome.* Arlington, TX: Future Horizons.

Weiss, R. P. (2000, July). Brain-based learning: The wave of the brain. *Training & Development,* 20–24. Retrieved from http://www.dushkin.com/text-data/articles/32638/body.pdf

Wiggins, G., & McTighe, J. (1998). *Understanding by design.* Alexandria, VA: Association for Supervision and Curriculum Development.

Winebrenner, S. (2006). *Teaching kids with learning difficulties in the regular classroom.* Minneapolis, MN: Free Spirit Publishing.

Wood, D. J., Bruner, J., & Ross, G. (1976). The role of tutoring in problem solving. *Journal of Child Psychology and Psychiatry, 17*(2), 89–100.

Wormeli, R. (2005). *Summarization in any subject.* Alexandria, VA: Association for Supervision and Curriculum Development.

Research Sources Supporting the Six Scaffolding Strategies

This table lists some of the publications by researchers and experts that support each of the six scaffolding strategies presented in chapter 5. This is not meant to be an exhaustive list of sources. Full citations are in the References section of this guidebook. Two of the publications listed in this table — Marzano, Pickering, and Pollock (2001) and Hill and Flynn (2006) — present findings from meta-analyses of extant research studies, so these two subsume many other studies. Sources that appear between the columns for English Learners and Learning Difficulties denote that the authors address both types of students.

	All Students	**English Learners**	**Learning Difficulties**
Visuals	Institute for the Advancement of Research in Education 2003 (S) Marzano, Pickering, & Pollock 2001 (S) Moore & Readence 1984 (S)	Gersten, Baker, & Marks 1998 (E) Hill & Flynn 2006 (S)	Anderson-Inman, Knox-Quinn, & Horney 1996 (R) Boyle & Weishaar 1997 (R) Bulgren, Schumaker, & Deschler 1988 (R) DiCecco & Gleason 2002 (R) Hudson, Lignugaris-Kraft, & Miller 1993 (S) Kim et al. 2004 (S) Mastropieri & Scruggs 1998 (R) Scanlon, Deshler, & Schumaker 1996 (R) Scruggs et al. 2009 (S) Winebrenner 2006 (E)
		Hall & Strangman 2002 (S) Thurlow et al. 2008 (E)	

(R) = Research
(S) = Synthesis of research
(E) = Expert advice, surveys, teacher focus groups

	All Students	**English Learners**	**Learning Difficulties**
Think-Pair-Share (Group Work)	Frey, Fisher, & Everlove 2009 (R) Lyman 1992 (E) Marzano, Pickering, & Pollock 2001 (S) Wormeli 2005 (E)	Diaz-Rico & Weed 2002 (R) Gibbons 2002 (R) Hill & Flynn 2006 (S)	Scruggs et al. 2009 (S) Winebrenner 2006 (E)
KWL+		Albus, Thurlow, & Clapper 2007 (R)	
		Gersten, Baker, & Marks 1998 (E)	Winebrenner 2006 (E)
Cues	Frey, Fisher, & Everlove 2009 (R) Lyman 1992 (E) Marzano, Pickering, & Pollock 2001 (S) Wormeli 2005 (E)	Diaz-Rico & Weed 2002 (R) Gibbons 2002 (R) Hill & Flynn 2006 (S)	Winebrenner 2006 (E)
Think Aloud	Bereiter & Bird 1985 (R) Pressley & Afflerbach 1995 (S)	Barrera et al. 2006 (R, mathematics) Thurlow et al. 2008 (E, mathematics)	
			Winebrenner 2006 (E)
Summarizing	Marzano, Pickering, & Pollock 2001 (S) Wormeli 2005 (E)	Hill & Flynn 2006 (S)	Lovitt et al. 1985 (E) Scruggs et al. 2009 (S) Winebrenner 2006 (E)
		Thurlow et al. 2008 (E, reading)	

(R) = Research
(S) = Synthesis of research
(E) = Expert advice, surveys, teacher focus groups

Appendix B

Common Core English Language Arts Standards on Comprehension and Collaboration

These standards are part of the Common Core State Standards developed by the Council of Chief State School Officers and the National Governors Association Center for Best Practices. More information is available from http://www.corestandards.org.

SPEAKING AND LISTENING STANDARDS: COMPREHENSION AND COLLABORATION, GRADES K–2		
Kindergarten	**Grade 1**	**Grade 2**
1. Participate in collaborative conversations with diverse partners about *kindergarten topics and texts* with peers and adults in small and larger groups. a. Follow agreed-upon rules for discussions (e.g., listening to others and taking turns speaking about the topics and texts under discussion). b. Continue a conversation through multiple exchanges. 2. Confirm understanding of a text read aloud or information presented orally or through other media by asking and answering questions about key details and requesting clarification if something is not understood. 3. Ask and answer questions in order to seek help, get information, or clarify something that is not understood.	1. Participate in collaborative conversations with diverse partners about *grade 1 topics and texts* with peers and adults in small and larger groups. a. Follow agreed-upon rules for discussions (e.g., listening to others with care, speaking one at a time about the topics and texts under discussion). b. Build on others' talk in conversations by responding to the comments of others through multiple exchanges. c. Ask questions to clear up any confusion about the topics and texts under discussion. 2. Ask and answer questions about key details in a text read aloud or information presented orally or through other media. 3. Ask and answer questions about what a speaker says in order to gather additional information or clarify something that is not understood.	1. Participate in collaborative conversations with diverse partners about *grade 2 topics and texts* with peers and adults in small and larger groups. a. Follow agreed-upon rules for discussions (e.g., gaining the floor in respectful ways, listening to others with care, speaking one at a time about the topics and texts under discussion). b. Build on others' talk in conversations by linking their comments to the remarks of others. c. Ask for clarification and further explanation as needed about the topics and texts under discussion. 2. Recount or describe key ideas or details from a text read aloud or information presented orally or through other media. 3. Ask and answer questions about what a speaker says in order to clarify comprehension, gather additional information, or deepen understanding of a topic or issue.

SPEAKING AND LISTENING STANDARDS: COMPREHENSION AND COLLABORATION, GRADES 3–5		
Grade 3	**Grade 4**	**Grade 5**
1. Engage effectively in a range of collaborative discussions (one-on-one, in groups, and teacher led) with diverse partners on *grade 3 topics and texts*, building on others' ideas and expressing their own clearly. a. Come to discussions prepared, having read or studied required material; explicitly draw on that preparation and other information known about the topic to explore ideas under discussion. b. Follow agreed-upon rules for discussions (e.g., gaining the floor in respectful ways, listening to others with care, speaking one at a time about the topics and texts under discussion). c. Ask questions to check understanding of information presented, stay on topic, and link their comments to the remarks of others. d. Explain their own ideas and understanding in light of the discussion. 2. Determine the main ideas and supporting details of a text read aloud or information presented in diverse media and formats, including visually, quantitatively, and orally. 3. Ask and answer questions about information from a speaker, offering appropriate elaboration and detail.	1. Engage effectively in a range of collaborative discussions (one-on-one, in groups, and teacher led) with diverse partners on *grade 4 topics and texts*, building on others' ideas and expressing their own clearly. a. Come to discussions prepared, having read or studied required material; explicitly draw on that preparation and other information known about the topic to explore ideas under discussion. b. Follow agreed-upon rules for discussions and carry out assigned roles. c. Pose and respond to specific questions to clarify or follow up on information, and make comments that contribute to the discussion and link to the remarks of others. d. Review the key ideas expressed and explain their own ideas and understanding in light of the discussion. 2. Paraphrase portions of a text read aloud or information presented in diverse media and formats, including visually, quantitatively, and orally. 3. Identify the reasons and evidence a speaker provides to support particular points.	1. Engage effectively in a range of collaborative discussions (one-on-one, in groups, and teacher led) with diverse partners on *grade 5 topics and texts*, building on others' ideas and expressing their own clearly. a. Come to discussions prepared, having read or studied required material; explicitly draw on that preparation and other information known about the topic to explore ideas under discussion. b. Follow agreed-upon rules for discussions and carry out assigned roles. c. Pose and respond to specific questions by making comments that contribute to the discussion and elaborate on the remarks of others. d. Review the key ideas expressed and draw conclusions in light of information and knowledge gained from the discussions. 2. Summarize a written text read aloud or information presented in diverse media and formats, including visually, quantitatively, and orally. 3. Summarize the points a speaker makes and explain how each claim is supported by reasons and evidence.

SPEAKING AND LISTENING STANDARDS: COMPREHENSION AND COLLABORATION, GRADES 6–8

Grade 6	Grade 7	Grade 8
1. Engage effectively in a range of collaborative discussions (one-on-one, in groups, and teacher led) with diverse partners on *grade 6 topics, texts, and issues,* building on others' ideas and expressing their own clearly.	1. Engage effectively in a range of collaborative discussions (one-on-one, in groups, and teacher led) with diverse partners on *grade 7 topics, texts, and issues,* building on others' ideas and expressing their own clearly.	1. Engage effectively in a range of collaborative discussions (one-on-one, in groups, and teacher led) with diverse partners on *grade 8 topics, texts, and issues,* building on others' ideas and expressing their own clearly.
a. Come to discussions prepared, having read or studied required material; explicitly draw on that preparation by referring to evidence on the topic, text, or issue to probe and reflect on ideas under discussion.	a. Come to discussions prepared, having read or researched material under study; explicitly draw on that preparation by referring to evidence on the topic, text, or issue to probe and reflect on ideas under discussion.	a. Come to discussions prepared, having read or researched material under study; explicitly draw on that preparation by referring to evidence on the topic, text, or issue to probe and reflect on ideas under discussion.
b. Follow rules for collegial discussions, set specific goals and deadlines, and define individual roles as needed.	b. Follow rules for collegial discussions, track progress toward specific goals and deadlines, and define individual roles as needed.	b. Follow rules for collegial discussions and decision-making, track progress toward specific goals and deadlines, and define individual roles as needed.
c. Pose and respond to specific questions with elaboration and detail by making comments that contribute to the topic, text, or issue under discussion.	c. Pose questions that elicit elaboration and respond to others' questions and comments with relevant observations and ideas that bring the discussion back on topic as needed.	c. Pose questions that connect the ideas of several speakers and respond to others' questions and comments with relevant evidence, observations, and ideas.
d. Review the key ideas expressed and demonstrate understanding of multiple perspectives through reflection and paraphrasing.	d. Acknowledge new information expressed by others and, when warranted, modify their own views.	d. Acknowledge new information expressed by others, and, when warranted, qualify or justify their own views in light of the evidence presented.
2. Interpret information presented in diverse media and formats (e.g., visually, quantitatively, orally) and explain how it contributes to a topic, text, or issue under study.	2. Analyze the main ideas and supporting details presented in diverse media and formats (e.g., visually, quantitatively, orally) and explain how the ideas clarify a topic, text, or issue under study.	2. Analyze the purpose of information presented in diverse media and formats (e.g., visually, quantitatively, orally) and evaluate the motives (e.g., social, commercial, political) behind its presentation.
3. Delineate a speaker's argument and specific claims, distinguishing claims that are supported by reasons and evidence from claims that are not.	3. Delineate a speaker's argument and specific claims, evaluating the soundness of the reasoning and the relevance and sufficiency of the evidence.	3. Delineate a speaker's argument and specific claims, evaluating the soundness of the reasoning and relevance and sufficiency of the evidence and identifying when irrelevant evidence is introduced.

SPEAKING AND LISTENING STANDARDS: COMPREHENSION AND COLLABORATION, GRADES 9–12

Grades 9–10	Grades 11–12
1. Initiate and participate effectively in a range of collaborative discussions (one-on-one, in groups, and teacher-led) with diverse partners on *grades 9–10 topics, texts, and issues,* building on others' ideas and expressing their own clearly and persuasively.	1. Initiate and participate effectively in a range of collaborative discussions (one-on-one, in groups, and teacher-led) with diverse partners on *grades 11–12 topics, texts, and issues,* building on others' ideas and expressing their own clearly and persuasively.
a. Come to discussions prepared, having read and researched material under study; explicitly draw on that preparation by referring to evidence from texts and other research on the topic or issue to stimulate a thoughtful, well-reasoned exchange of ideas.	a. Come to discussions prepared, having read and researched material under study; explicitly draw on that preparation by referring to evidence from texts and other research on the topic or issue to stimulate a thoughtful, well reasoned exchange of ideas.
b. Work with peers to set rules for collegial discussions and decision-making (e.g., informal consensus, taking votes on key issues, presentation of alternate views), clear goals and deadlines, and individual roles as needed.	b. Work with peers to promote civil, democratic discussions and decision making, set clear goals and deadlines, and establish individual roles as needed.
c. Propel conversations by posing and responding to questions that relate the current discussion to broader themes or larger ideas; actively incorporate others into the discussion; and clarify, verify, or challenge ideas and conclusions.	c. Propel conversations by posing and responding to questions that probe reasoning and evidence; ensure a hearing for a full range of positions on a topic or issue; clarify, verify, or challenge ideas and conclusions; and promote divergent and creative perspectives.
d. Respond thoughtfully to diverse perspectives, summarize points of agreement and disagreement, and, when warranted, qualify or justify their own views and understanding and make new connections in light of the evidence and reasoning presented.	d. Respond thoughtfully to diverse perspectives; synthesize comments, claims, and evidence made on all sides of an issue; solve contradictions when possible; and determine what additional information or research is required to deepen the investigation or complete the task.
2. Integrate multiple sources of information presented in diverse media or formats (e.g., visually, quantitatively, orally) evaluating the credibility and accuracy of each source.	2. Integrate multiple sources of information presented in diverse formats and media (e.g., visually, quantitatively, orally) in order to make informed decisions and solve problems, evaluating the credibility and accuracy of each source and noting any discrepancies among the data.
3. Evaluate a speaker's point of view, reasoning, and use of evidence and rhetoric, identifying any fallacious reasoning or exaggerated or distorted evidence.	3. Evaluate a speaker's point of view, reasoning, and use of evidence and rhetoric, assessing the stance, premises, links among ideas, word choice, points of emphasis, and tone used.

Index

About the Authors

JOHN W. CARR develops resources, conducts workshops, and evaluates educational programs. He developed WestEd's bestselling *Map of Standards for English Learners* and conducts supportive workshops that assist teachers in implementing standards-based instruction for English learners. He coauthored a WestEd best-seller series of guidebooks — *Making Science Accessible to English Learners: A Guidebook for Teachers* (2007) and *Making Mathematics Accessible to English Learners: A Guidebook for Teachers* (2009). This guidebook is the third in the series, extending the approach to students with learning difficulties. He conducts professional development on standards-based instruction for English learners and students in inclusive classrooms.

He has conducted a variety of instructional program evaluations regarding refugee students, English learners, and students with special needs. His current interest is in research-based instructional practices for students with learning difficulties in academic classes and the evaluation of special education programs. John has a PhD in measurement, evaluation, and research methodology from the University of California, Berkeley. He worked in the research and evaluation departments of two large school districts for 13 years and conducted workshops on school improvement. John is currently a Senior Research Associate in the Evaluation Research Program at WestEd. He can be contacted at jcarr@WestEd.org.

SHAREN BERTRANDO develops materials and provides training, resources, and technical assistance for projects such as the Least Restrictive Environment Resources Project, Po'okela Project Centers of Educational Excellence on Inclusive Practices and Access to the Common Core, and the Windward District Achievement4All Restructuring Project. In addition, she provides technical assistance and training to support diverse learners using technology as an effective instructional tool. She works with the California Comprehensive Center and the California Department of Education to develop educational resources to support students with disabilities, including second language learners with disabilities.

Sharen is currently a member of the California Autism Training Team with the National Professional Development Center — ASD and the California Community of Practice Secondary Transition Leadership Team. Sharen has more than 20 years of experience as a teacher and program coordinator in California and Oregon. She has a diverse educational background and professional experience educating students, from preschoolers to adolescents.

Sharen's current position is as a Special Education Resource Development Specialist in WestEd's Center for Prevention and Early Intervention. She can be contacted at sbertra@WestEd.org.

Also Available
from WestEd

Making Science Accessible to English Learners
A Guidebook for Teachers, Updated Edition

John Carr, Ursula Sexton, and Rachel Lagunoff

This updated edition of the best-selling guidebook helps upper elementary, middle, and high school science teachers who have had limited preparation for teaching science in classrooms where some students are also English learners. Teachers receive powerful and concrete strategies to help English learners engage with the language and processes of science, including:

» Rubrics to help identify the most important language skills at five ELD levels

» Practical guidance and tips from the field

» Seven scaffolding strategies for differentiating instruction

» Seven tools to promote academic language and scientific discourse

» Assessment techniques and accommodations to lower communication barriers

» Two integrated lesson scenarios that can be used immediately

$24.95 • 132 pages • Trade paper • 8.5 x 11 • 2007 • 978-0-914409-40-3 • CC-07-01B

Read sample chapters at WestEd.org/makingscienceaccessible.

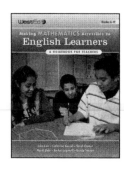

Making Mathematics Accessible to English Learners
A Guidebook for Teachers

John Carr, Catherine Carroll, Sarah Cremer, Mardi Gale, Rachel Lagunoff, and Ursula Sexton

Designed for upper elementary, middle, and high school mathematics teachers who have had limited preparation for teaching mathematics to English learners, this guide offers an integrated approach to teaching mathematics content and English language skills.

Teachers receive:

» Rubrics to help identify the most important language skills at five ELD levels

» Practical guidance and tips from the field

» Seven scaffolding strategies for differentiating instruction

» Seven tools to promote mathematical language

» Assessment techniques and accommodations to lower communication barriers

» Three integrated lesson scenarios that can be used immediately

$24.95 • 128 pages • Trade paper • 8.5 x 11 • 2009 • 978-0-914409-68-7 • CC-09-01B

Read a sample chapter at WestEd.org/makingmathematicsaccessible.

For more information about WestEd's research and services or to sign up to receive our monthly e-bulletin, visit WestEd.org. To order books and other products, visit WestEd.org/bookstore or call us toll-free at 888.293.7833.

Professional Development from WestEd

Making Science Accessible to English Learners
Professional Development

Who Should Participate

» Science teachers grades 4–12

» Secondary-level English language development and science leaders, coaches, and staff developers

What Participants Learn

Using the principles and approaches described in *Making Science Accessible to English Learners: A Guidebook for Teachers, Updated Edition*, WestEd offers professional development for schools and districts to work into an existing and ongoing professional support system for teachers. Participants enhance their knowledge and skills to plan and differentiate instruction and assessment for diverse learners, particularly English learners.

Participants learn:

» How to engage English learners in scientific discourse and practice in order to successfully learn science content, literacy, and communication skills

» How to embed teaching strategies that are highly effective for English learners in an inquiry-based approach to teaching science

» What to expect of English learners at each level of language acquisition

» How to apply tools and strategies for building vocabulary and literacy, and planning lessons that engage all learners

» How to use strategies for teaching and applying academic language throughout each lesson and how to build a cohesive unit of lessons

» How to integrate seven research-based strategies as scaffolds to rigorous content standards

» How to design appropriate assessments for English learners

Format

A two- and three-day professional development can be tailored with flexible dates for school or district teams of up to 35 people.

The two-day workshop engages participants in a hands-on, student-centered model lesson, and offers the opportunity to delve deeper into how to effectively integrate research-based strategies that are highly effective for English learners. Participants integrate tools and strategies into doable discipline-specific lessons, with many opportunities to explore, inquire, reflect, and problem solve with each other and the facilitator about practical ways to refine their practice. Participants explore designing cohesive lessons and managing a student-centered classroom with adaptations for English learners.

The three-day workshop also includes formative assessment design strategies to align and inform instruction, making science instruction culturally relevant to students. The workshop can be a summer institute of consecutive days or interspersed throughout the school year, allowing participants to experiment with this teaching approach between workshop sessions.

Contact Ursula Sexton at **usexton@WestEd.org** for more information.

Professional Development from WestEd

Making Mathematics Accessible to English Learners
Professional Development

Who Should Participate

» Mathematics teachers grades 4–12

» Mathematics coaches, instructional leaders, and staff developers

What Participants Learn

Using the principles and approaches described in *Making Mathematics Accessible to English Learners: A Guidebook for Teachers,* WestEd offers professional development for schools and districts. Participants enhance their knowledge and skills to differentiate instruction and assessment for diverse learners, particularly English learners, thereby giving all students universal, equitable access to a rigorous mathematics curriculum.

Participants learn how to:

» Tailor the three-phase model of mathematics instruction to support an inquiry-based approach to teaching English learners

» Use a chart of eight essential language skills to plan lessons that include English learners at different language development levels

» Apply academic language during mathematics lessons

» Design accommodations to create equitable classroom mathematics assessments

» Implement seven research-based strategies to scaffold rigorous mathematics content standards

» Integrate the instructional tools and strategies into doable daily pedagogy

Format

Two-day professional development workshops with flexible dates are available for school or district teams of up to 35 people.

Contact Cathy Carroll at **ccarrol@WestEd.org** for more information.

Also Available from WestEd

Making Sense of SCIENCE™

"This has been the most beneficial and relevant course I have taken! It directly relates to what I am teaching … It was fabulous!"

— Stephanie Werdin, Classroom Teacher, Madison, Wisconsin

Making Sense of SCIENCE offers a comprehensive series of professional development courses that focus on core topics of K–8 earth, life, and physical science. Each course provides the necessary ingredients for building a scientific way of thinking in teachers and students by focusing on science content, inquiry, and literacy.

Teachers who participate in these courses learn to facilitate hands-on science lessons, support evidence-based discussions, and develop students' academic language and literacy skills in science, along with the habits of mind necessary for sense making and scientific reasoning.

Available Now

Energy for Teachers of Grades 6–8

Two paperback books and two CD-ROMs

$249.95 • 656 pages
Multimedia • 8.5 x 11
2011 • 978-0-914409-78-6
MSS-11-02B

Force & Motion for Teachers of Grades 6–8

Two paperback books and two CD-ROMs

$249.95 • 656 pages
Multimedia • 8.5 x 11
2011 • 978-0-914409-77-9
MSS-11-01B

Matter for Teachers of Grades 6–8

Two paperback books and two CD-ROMs

$249.95 • 656 pages
Multimedia • 8.5 x 11
2012 • 978-1-938287-02-2
MSS-12-01B

Coming Soon

For Teachers of Grades 3–5

>> Magnetism
>> Earth's Systems
>> Electric Circuits
>> Earth's Organisms

For Teachers of Grades 6–8

>> Plate Tectonics
>> Weather & Climate
>> Heredity & Selection

Visit WestEd.org/mss for more information.

Published in partnership with

NSTApress
National Science Teachers Association

For more information about WestEd's research and services or to sign up to receive our monthly e-bulletin, visit WestEd.org. To order books and other products, visit WestEd.org/bookstore or call us toll-free at 888.293.7833.

Professional Development from WestEd

Teaching English Learners and Students With Learning Difficulties in an Inclusive Classroom Professional Development

Who Should Participate

» Teachers and specialists who provide academic instruction to English learners and/or students with learning difficulties in grades 6–12 (may include lower grades)

» Teacher support staff such as staff developers, specialists, and coaches

» School/district teams of general and special education instructional leaders, teacher support staff, and teachers for gradual school implementation

» Whole school academic instructional staff for immediate school implementation

Goals of the Workshop

Participants attain the knowledge and practice the skills to implement a doable, daily, research-based set of specific strategies to tailor academic instruction for English learners and students with learning difficulties such as specific learning disabilities, ADHD, and Asperger's syndrome.

School/district teams attain the knowledge, practice the skills, and plan to implement the strategies schoolwide, blending this approach with other improvement initiatives and prior professional development.

What You Learn

» The language skills of English learners at different developmental levels to learn and communicate what they have learned

» The learning characteristics of students with prevalent learning difficulties

» How to blend direct instruction and inquiry-based, student-led learning for all diverse learners

» How to develop academic vocabulary and discourse in a discipline for all diverse learners

» How to integrate six strategies to scaffold content learning for all diverse learners

» How to assess content learning in the classroom for all diverse learners

» How to "put it all together" as a doable, daily approach to teaching in an inclusive classroom

What Resources Support Your Learning

The workshop is based on *Teaching English Learners and Students with Learning Difficulties in an Inclusive Classroom: A Guidebook for Teachers*, written by workshop leaders John Carr and Sharen Bertrando.

Cost

The on-site, one-day workshop covers the fundamentals and costs $4,000 for up to 35 participants.

The on-site, two-day workshop with flexible dates offers more intensive exploration, application, and team planning time, and costs $8,000 for up to 35 participants. Travel costs are separate.

Participants receive a 30% discount off the list price of *Teaching English Learners and Students with Learning Difficulties in an Inclusive Classroom: A Guidebook for Teachers*.

Contact John Carr at **jcarr@WestEd.org** for more information.